NICK AND TE~

HIGP
D.

"SCIENCE BOB" P.   reaches elementary
school science in New   Massachusetts.

STEVE HOCKENSMITH writes mysteries in Alameda,
California. Neither author was harmed during the
creation of this book.

NICK AND TESLA'S
HIGH-VOLTAGE DANGER LAB

A MYSTERY WITH ELECTROMAGNETS, BURGLAR ALARMS, AND OTHER GADGETS YOU CAN BUILD YOURSELF

"SCIENCE BOB" PFLUGFELDER
AND STEVE HOCKENSMITH

ILLUSTRATIONS BY SCOTT GARRETT

RED TURTLE
RUPA

Published in Red Turtle by
Rupa Publications India Pvt. Ltd 2016
7/16, Ansari Road, Daryaganj
New Delhi 110002

Sales centres:
Allahabad Bengaluru Chennai
Hyderabad Jaipur Kathmandu
Kolkata Mumbai

Text Copyright © Quirk Productions, Inc 2013

Designed by Doogie Horner
Illustrations by Scott Garrett

First published in United States of America by Quirk Productions, Inc.
This edition published by arrangement with the original publisher.

This is a work of fiction. Names, characters, places and incidents are either
the product of the author's imagination or are used fictitiously, and any
resemblance to any actual persons, living or dead,
events or locales is entirely coincidental.

ISBN: 978-81-291-4202-3

First impression 2016

10 9 8 7 6 5 4 3 2 1

DANGER! DANGER!
DANGER! DANGER!

The how-to projects in this book involve electricity, explosions, toxic substances, sharp tools, contents under pressure, and other potentially dangerous elements. Before you build any of the projects, ASK AN ADULT TO REVIEW THE INSTRUCTIONS. You'll probably need their help with one or two of the steps, anyway.

While we believe these projects to be safe and family-friendly, accidents can happen in any situation, and we cannot guarantee your safety. THE AUTHORS AND PUBLISHER DISCLAIM ANY LIABILITY FROM ANY HARM OR INJURY THAT MAY RESULT FROM THE USE, PROPER OR IMPROPER, OF THE INFORMATION CONTAINED IN THIS BOOK. Remember, the instructions in this book are not meant to be a substitute for your good judgment and common sense.

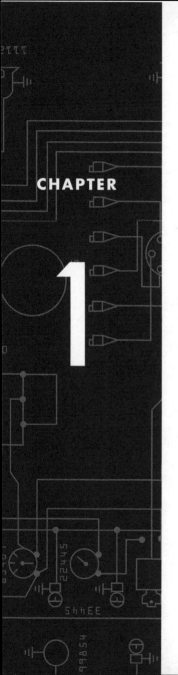

1

Someone climbed into Joe Devlin's cab, and he put down his newspaper and looked in the rearview mirror and started to say "Where to?"

He froze.

Sitting behind him were a boy and a girl with sad, serious expressions on their faces. They looked like they were eleven or twelve years old.

There were no adults in sight.

Two kids getting into a taxi, alone, outside San Francisco International Airport?

Trouble, Joe's gut said.

The boy looked down at a letter

he was holding.

"Five-thirteen Chesterfield Avenue," he said.

Joe could hear the paper rustling as he spoke. The boy's hands were shaking.

"In Half Moon Bay," the girl said, her voice firm, resolute. "That's near here, right?"

Joe turned around to squint at his would-be passengers. They were dressed like any other kids—T-shirts, jeans, sneakers—yet they seemed subdued and grave in a way that didn't fit their ages. All they had with them were the letter and two small, black suitcases and a book each.

The boy was holding something called *A Brief History of Time*. The girl had *Theory of Applied Robotics: Kinematics, Dynamics, and Control.*

"You're not running away, are you?" Joe said. "Where are your parents?"

"No, we're not runaways," the girl said. "Our parents are . . . well . . ."

"They're in Uzbekistan," said the boy.

Joe blinked.

"Uzbekistan?" he said.

The boy nodded. "Watching soybeans grow."

"Well," the girl said, "it's a little more complicated

than that."

"Oh," said Joe. "Ooooooookay."

"We've been sent to live with our uncle for the summer," the boy said. "He was supposed to meet us here, but he didn't show up."

Joe stared at the kids a moment, trying to decide if he believed them. Even if he did, they still looked like trouble. And Joe didn't like trouble.

The girl stuffed a hand into the pocket of her jeans and pulled out a wad of wrinkled bills.

"We have ninety-three dollars," she said.

The boy reached into his pocket, too. "And fifty-eight cents. That's enough, right?"

"Absolutely," Joe said.

He turned around and started the engine. And the meter.

Joe didn't like trouble. But he did like money.

Every so often, Joe stole a peek at the kids in the rearview mirror. The girl was watching the rolling Northern California hills slide by. The boy was toying with a silver pendant he wore on a chain around his

neck. It was shaped like a star.

"Stop that," the girl said when she noticed what her brother was doing. "You might break it."

"Break what? I still haven't even figured out what it is."

"It's jewelry, that's all. A keepsake from Mom and Dad."

"Since when have Mom and Dad been into keep-sakes?"

The girl shrugged.

The boy started picking at the pendant again.

"Anyway," he muttered, "I don't wear jewelry."

The girl went back to staring out the window.

After a moment, though, she pulled out an identical pendant hanging around her neck and began rubbing it absentmindedly.

About twenty yards behind her, Joe noticed, was a big, black SUV that had been following them for miles. It was probably just a coincidence that it had stayed with them as they went from the airport to 101 South to 92 West. But then again, if Trouble had to drive, wouldn't it drive a big, black SUV?

Joe gave his cab a little more gas.

Joe made the winding drive down to Half Moon Bay at least once a week. Though it was just a speck of a city, it was perfectly situated—nestled on the coast at the edge of a long stretch of lush, hilly forest—and had built up a healthy tourist trade. The town itself was quiet and quaint and cute. And boring, but the tourists didn't seem to mind.

Five-thirteen Chesterfield Avenue was in a nice neighborhood not far from the ocean. The house looked a little shabby, though. The paint was more faded, the driveway more cracked, the yard more choked with weeds than any of its neighbors. Even the mailbox was dented and scorched on one side.

As Joe's cab slowed to a stop out front, a lawn mower was going around and around in the yard. No one was going around and around behind it, though. It looked like a ghost was mowing the lawn.

Rope ran from the mower to a metal pole in the middle of the yard. The end of the rope was wrapped around the top of the pole in a coil. As the mower moved, the rope unraveled itself, slowly feeding more slack to the mower so it could go in bigger and bigger circles.

It was a self-mowing lawn.

"Cool," said the girl.

"Uhh," said the boy.

He pointed to the pole. The more the mower tugged on it, the more it tilted to the side.

"Oh," said the girl.

The pole sagged, then fell over completely, and the mower rumbled off-course into a neighboring yard. It chewed through row after row of beautifully manicured flowers before rolling over a garden gnome, getting snagged, and—with a screech and a *pop* and a puff of black smoke—bursting into flames.

"Well," the girl said, "cool *idea*."

"Sixty-five dollars," Joe said.

The girl counted out the money.

"And we're supposed to tip you, right?" the boy said.

"Don't worry about it," said Joe. His conscience was yelling at him not to abandon a couple of kids outside a run-down house with an exploding lawn mower. He needed to leave quick or he might actually listen.

He glanced at the kids in his rearview mirror as he sped away. They were kneeling beside the fallen pole examining the rope. They looked like they wanted to put the pole back up, find another mower, and try again.

A little farther down the street, Joe could see the black SUV he'd noticed behind them on the highway. A shadowy figure sat behind the wheel. Whoever it was, he or she seemed to be watching the kids.

Joe's gut had been right about those two. They were trouble. *Weird* trouble.

As he drove away, fast, Joe made a promise to

himself that he planned to keep the next time he was at the airport.

From now on, middle-aged tourists only. Middle-aged tourists only. Middle-aged tourists only. . . .

"At least we know Uncle Newt's around here somewhere," Tesla said.

"How do we know that?" asked her brother Nick.

Tesla nodded at the lawn mower. "Who do you think started that?"

"That doesn't prove anything," Nick said. "If you could rig it to mow by itself, you could rig it to start itself, too."

"True. Want to go check for a timer?"

The lawn mower wasn't burning anymore, but the engine still sizzled and smoldered ominously.

"Maybe later," Nick said.

"All right then."

Tesla picked up her suitcase and started toward the house. She'd taken it upon herself to be the leader lately. She was the elder sibling, after all.

She'd been born twelve minutes before her twin

brother.

Nick got his own suitcase and followed her onto the porch.

Tesla started to reach for the doorbell. It chimed when her finger was still two feet from the button.

"Hey," Tesla said, looking around the porch.

Nick looked, too.

"Motion detector?" he said.

"Could be."

Tesla was standing on a welcome mat. Printed on it were the words IF YOU'RE SELLING GIRL SCOUT COOKIES, I'M NOT HOME.

Tesla noticed a wire running from the mat to the door frame. She stepped off the mat, then back on.

The doorbell chimed again.

"Pressure sensor," Nick said. "Nice."

"Yeah. Only, if Uncle Newt's so smart, how come he wasn't at the airport?"

"Mom and Dad always said he was a little . . . off. Maybe he just forgot."

"Forgot that his niece and nephew were coming today to live with him?"

Nick gave his sister a sad, weary shrug.

Their summer was off to a pretty lousy start. Two

days out of school and *bang*—their trip to Disneyland is canceled, their scientist parents tell them they have to rush to Central Asia to observe dramatic new soybean irrigation techniques, and they're shipped off to live with the reclusive uncle no one else in the family can talk about without smirking or shivering.

Fun in the sun it was not.

Tesla sighed.

"We're not here to sell you Girl Scout cookies!" she called out.

Still no one came to the door.

Tesla reached for the knob. The door wasn't locked.

Tesla opened it.

"Are you sure you should do that?" Nick said.

"Why not?" Tesla stepped inside. "This is supposedly our house now, too. For the next three months anyway."

"But . . . what if Uncle Newt has, like, a vicious attack dog?"

"Then it would've started barking the second the doorbell rang."

"Oh. Right."

Tesla moved deeper into the darkness of the

house.

Nick stayed on the porch.

"What in the—? My begonias!" he heard someone say behind him.

Nick looked over his shoulder.

A small but muscular woman in sweaty workout clothes was stepping out of a big shiny car in the neighbor's driveway. She was gaping in horror at the chewed-up flowerbed and the smoking lawn mower.

Scowling, she turned toward Uncle Newt's house. And the scowl didn't go away when she noticed Nick looking back at her. In fact, it got scowlier.

Nick smiled weakly, waved, and hurried into the house. He closed the door behind him.

"Whoa," he said when his eyes adjusted to the gloom inside.

Cluttering the long hall in front of him were dozens of old computers, a telescope, a metal detector connected to a pair of bulky earphones, an old-fashioned diving suit complete with brass helmet, a stuffed polar bear (the real, dead kind), a chainsaw, something that looked like a flamethrower (but couldn't be . . . right?), a box marked KEEP REFRIGERATED, another marked THIS END UP (upside down), and a fully lit Christmas tree decorated with ornaments made from broken beakers and test tubes (it was June). Exposed wires and power cables poked out of the plaster and veered off around every corner, and there were so many diplomas and science prizes and patents hanging (all of them earned by Newton Galileo Holt, a.k.a. Uncle Newt) that barely an inch of wall was left uncovered.

Off to the left was a living room lined with enough books to put some libraries to shame, a semi-transparent couch made of inflated plastic bags, and a wide-screen TV connected by frayed cords to a small trampoline. The ceiling over the trampoline was cracked and cratered, as if someone kept bouncing a little too high. A dented football helmet was lying nearby on the floor.

To Nick's right was a dining room with a conveyor belt running to the kitchen, a gas grill built into the middle of the table, and straps and buckles hanging from the ceiling, instead of chairs.

Tesla was petting a hairless cat that stood on the table licking the frosting off a chocolate cake. As Nick came closer, he saw words written with yellow icing.

WELCOME
ICK AND TESLA

The cat had eaten the N.

"So Uncle Newt *didn't* forget we were coming," Nick said.

"Apparently not," said Tesla.

"Where is he, then?"

Tesla gave the cat a scratch behind one hairless ear. The cat just kept licking at the cake, but now it was purring.

"I don't know," Tesla said. "Maybe the cat ate him, too."

Tesla cocked her head to the side.

"Hey," she said. "Do you hear something?"

Nick cocked his head just as his sister had, though he wondered why anyone bothered doing that.

Does lifting one ear at an approximately thirty-degree angle really increase one's ability to detect faint noises? he thought. Because he was that sort of kid.

Then he heard it.

"Someone's shouting," he said. "But I can't make out the words."

Tesla cocked her head even more and then bent

over, bringing her ear closer to the floor.

Nick did the same.

Without a word, Tesla walked out of the dining room and into the kitchen, still tilted to one side. Nick followed at an identical angle.

On the far side of the kitchen, beside the refrigerator, was a door. It was covered with signs.

KEEP OUT
PRIVATE PROPERTY
AUTHORIZED PERSONNEL ONLY
TRESPASSERS WILL BE PROSECUTED
HAZARDOUS
FLAMMABLE
POISON
HIGH VOLTAGE
DANGER
BEWARE OF DOG

The word DOG had been crossed out and replaced with CAT.

As Nick and Tesla crossed the kitchen, the muffled cries grew louder.

Tesla reached out and opened the door. Just beyond it was a dark stairwell.

Something at the bottom of the stairs hummed and glowed.

"HEEEEEEEEEEEELLLLLLLLLLLP!" someone said.

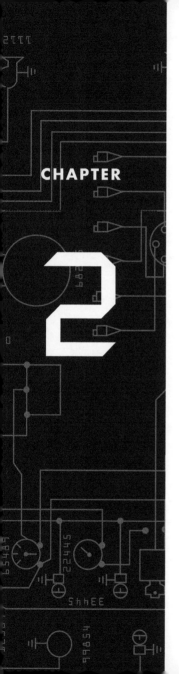

2

Tesla hurried down the stairs.

Nick started down the stairs, too, but didn't hurry. He was a look-before-you-leap kind of person. Which made him a look-before-you-rush-into-strange-basements marked-HIGH VOLTAGE-and-DAN-GER kind of person.

"Oh, yuck!" Tesla said when she was far enough down the stairs to get a look around. "What the heck is that?"

Her words didn't inspire Nick to move any faster.

"What the heck is what?" he said. But by then he was far enough down to see for himself.

Spread-eagle on the basement floor was the blobby orange outline of a man. It shone and glistened moistly in the dim, sputtering glow of the fluorescent lights hanging from the ceiling.

Then it spoke.

"Nick? Tesla? Is that you?"

"Uncle Newt?" Nick and Tesla said at the same time.

"Yes! Yes, it's me! You've got to help me!"

The kids moved cautiously toward the orange blob. (Well, Nick moved cautiously. Tesla just moved.)

The blob was in the middle of what was obviously a laboratory. Two worktables, arranged along the nearest walls, were covered with beakers, flasks, burners, scales, petri dishes, soldering irons, and electronics components both large and small, broken and unbroken. Mixed in with the standard lab equipment was some not-so-standard equipment, including a half-melted Easy Bake oven, a coffeepot filled with bubbling orange goo, and a trumpet, trombone, and saxophone welded together at the mouthpiece. Farther back, in the darker corners of the lab, was an array of shadowy shapes and blinking lights and things that went "bloop" and "fizz" and "ping."

Under normal circumstances, Tesla and Nick—both of them lovers of gadgets and contraptions and things that go "ping"—would have wandered off to explore with wide-eyed wonderment. But these weren't normal circumstances.

"I glued myself to the floor," Uncle Newt said.

Tesla kneeled beside the orange blob. It looked spongy yet dense.

"How can you breathe in there?" she said.

"Look down."

Tesla peered at the lower edge of the blob and then flattened herself on the floor to try to see what was under it.

"Oh," she said. "Hi."

Nick lay down, too. He could see a man's lips and nose and forehead smooshed into the cool cement floor beneath the blob. One blue eye blinked, or perhaps winked, at him.

"Hi," Nick said.

"Gosh," Uncle Newt said, "you've both gotten so big. How old are you again?"

"Eleven," Nick said.

"Eleven! Wow! The last time I saw you two, you

were practically babies, and now just look at you! Old enough to drive!"

"Uh . . . no," Nick said.

"Uncle Newt?" Tesla said.

"All right, almost old enough to drive," said Uncle Newt. "When can you get a learner's permit? When you're twelve?"

"Uh . . . no," Nick said.

"Uncle Newt?" Tesla said.

"Thirteen, then? Fourteen?" Uncle Newt said. "Anyway, we've got plenty of time to figure that out. First things first. Do you have your pilot's license?"

"Uh . . . no," Nick said.

"Uncle Newt," Tesla said. "How do we get you un-stuck?"

"Oh! Right! You need to find a spray bottle filled with purple liquid."

Nick and Tesla stood up and looked around. Nick spotted the bottle first. It was sitting beside the goo-filled coffeepot and another spray bottle, this one half full of something orange.

Nick picked up the bottle with the purple stuff inside.

"Got it," he said.

"Now what?" said Tesla.

"You spray me, of course!" said Uncle Newt.

Nick walked back over to the blob on the floor and began spritzing it uncertainly. The liquid in the bottle came out in a fine purple mist. It started blistering and bubbling as soon as it hit the orange whatever-it-was covering Uncle Newt.

"That's it. I can feel it loosening up," Uncle Newt said as the orange stuff collapsed and liquefied. "Squirt some more on my legs. Great. Now my shoulders. Perfect. Now a little on the back of my head. Right there! Yes!"

There was a *rrrrrrrrrrripping* sound, and Uncle Newt pushed himself off the floor and popped to his feet. No longer was he a just big orange splotch on the floor. Now he was a tall, thin, though still mostly orange, human being.

"Success!" he said.

Chunks of sludge were dripping from his back, and half the white lab coat he was wearing had torn away and remained stuck to the laboratory floor. Yet Uncle Newt was smiling.

Nick hadn't seen his uncle in years—they lived in Virginia, on the other side of the continent, and Dad always said his brother "didn't travel well"—but he remembered that smile. It was big and toothy and warm. And a little demented.

"Now how about a hug?" Uncle Newt said, spreading out arms wet with still-sizzling sludge.

"Maybe later?" Tesla said. "When you're a little less . . . toxic?"

"Good thinking."

Uncle Newt tried to take off what was left of his lab coat. It wasn't easy. Parts of it were still cemented to the T-shirt and jeans he wore underneath, and everything was coated in orange-purple ooze.

After some struggling, Uncle Newt gave up.

"Darn. I loved this T-shirt," he said. Sadly, he patted the words printed on it: NASA—YOU DON'T HAVE TO BE CRAZY TO WORK HERE, BUT THE ALIENS LIVING IN MY NOSE SAY IT HELPS. "Oh, well. It was probably time to get rid of it anyway. It's smelled like rotten broccoli for ten years now. Anyway, on to happier topics. How was your flight? I hope you weren't too bummed about suddenly leaving behind everything and everyone you've ever known."

"Well . . ." Nick began.

"Wait," said Tesla. "What is that orange gunk?

And how'd you get stuck to the floor in it?"

Uncle Newt's eyes lit up with excitement.

"'Gunk'?" he said, waving a hand at the goo on his back. "This isn't gunk! It's the future!"

Nick and Tesla looked at each other as Uncle Newt wobbled awkwardly toward the nearest work-table. (The back of his jeans was still coated in stiff orange foam.) Their father had always told them that his older brother was "a self-employed inventor." But it looked to Nick and Tesla like another job description would fit even better.

Their uncle was a mad scientist.

"Observe!" Uncle Newt said, snatching up the spray bottle filled with orange liquid and whirling around to face the kids (and nearly losing his balance again in the process). He pointed the bottle at the back of his left hand and squeezed.

Vapor shot from the nozzle and coated his skin in a layer of spongy orange. Uncle Newt kept spraying, turning his hand this way and that until it was covered evenly all the way around.

"What do you think I'll have once this dries?" he said.

"An orange hand?" Nick said.

"Yes. And . . .?"

"An orange *glove*," said Tesla, looking impressed.

Uncle Newt grinned, delighted.

"Exactly!" He shook the spray bottle. "Instant spray-on clothes!"

The spongy orange "glove" on Uncle Newt's hand kept expanding until it looked more like an orange mitten, and then a puffy orange boxing glove.

Uncle Newt's grin faded.

"Except I don't seem to have the formula quite right. It gets a little globby. And stiff. And sticky. I was

just trying to squeeze in one more quick full-body test before I went to the airport to get you, but, well, it didn't go so well."

It now looked like Uncle Newt had a basketball stuck to the end of his arm.

"Nick, could you give me a hand?"

"Right."

Nick stepped up with the other spray bottle and coated the blob with purple mist. It immediately began fizzing and melting.

"Hey!" Uncle Newt said. "The airport! Oh, my gosh! How'd you get here?"

"We took a cab," Tesla said.

Uncle Newt slapped a hand to his forehead, smearing it with orange slime.

"Oh, wow. I am so sorry. Believe me, kids, I take this responsibility very seriously. Wherever your parents are—"

"Uzbekistan," said Tesla.

"—and whatever they're doing—"

"Studying soybean irrigation," said Nick.

"—and whenever they're coming back—"

"Labor Day," Nick and Tesla said together.

"—I want you to know that you have nothing to

worry about. I won't fall down on the job again. I will always be there for you. Always. Now," Uncle Newt turned and headed toward the stairs, "I've got to go take a shower."

"Uh . . . what should *we* do?" Nick asked as his uncle went up the steps.

Uncle Newt didn't slow down.

"Oh, I don't know. Your father used to tell me you were following in our footsteps. Inventing, like him and me and your mom. Well, now there's nothing to hold you back. My laboratory is your laboratory. Go nuts!"

Nick and Tesla looked at each other. They'd never thought of their parents as inventors. They were staff horticulturists at the U.S. Department of Agriculture, which seemed like about the least inventive thing one could be.

Also, "go nuts" was not the kind of thing they were used to hearing from authority figures.

Uncle Newt stopped and pointed at an especially dark corner of the basement.

"Oh. Only, whatever you do, don't touch that. Or that. Or that." Uncle Newt began moving his hand here and there, though it was hard to tell exactly what he was pointing at. "Or that or that or that or that. And *definitely* don't touch that. Hoo boy! That stuff over there you could build yourself a rocket with. That stuff over there would melt a hole in the floor. Don't get 'em mixed up, okay? I'll see you in an hour or two."

"An hour or two?" Nick said.

Uncle Newt started up the stairs again.

"I am *really* dirty!"

And then he was gone.

Nick looked around the basement and said, "Great. We've got our own lab, and I'm afraid to touch a thing in it."

Tesla looked around the basement and said, "We've got our own lab! Woo-hoo!"

She walked over to a machine that had caught her eye: a hulking collection of pipes and wires and tubes and flashing lights.

"I don't remember," she said. "Was this a 'don't touch,' a '*definitely* don't touch,' or neither?"

"Uncle Newt didn't say. Which makes it a 'definitely don't touch,' in my book."

Tesla stepped up to a little porthole in the side of the mysterious mechanism.

"I wonder what this thing does?"

As Tesla leaned in to peer through the porthole, she brushed against a pair of handlebars. Or what she thought were handlebars. They moved downward with a loud *clack*.

The machine began to hum.

"Oh, man," Nick said.

The machine began to vibrate.

"Oh, man!" Nick said.

The machine began to hiss and spark and shake so hard it was practically jumping off the floor.

"Ohhhhhhhh, maaaaaaaan!" Nick said.

He and Tesla ran for cover.

They ducked behind what looked like a pile of garbage beside one of the work tables. When they peeked back at the machine, it was spitting out loose nuts and bolts and crackling curlicues of electricity.

"It's gonna blow!" Nick yelled. "*It's gonna blow!*"

"*Ding,*" said the machine. And nothing else.

Suddenly, it was totally silent, totally still.

The little porthole glowed with an eerie yellow light.

Tesla stood up and walked toward it.

"Tez," said Nick.

Tesla looked through the porthole, then reached up to touch it.

"Tez, don't."

There was a shallow groove in one side of the porthole glass. Tesla put her fingers in it, then pulled to the side.

The porthole slid open. Something small and dark sat in the chamber just beyond.

"Tez!" Nick said as his sister reached in and pulled the little something out.

It was a porcelain cup.

Tesla sniffed the steam rising up from it.

"Cappuccino," she said.

She put the cup back in the chamber and closed the porthole.

"So . . . it's a coffee maker?" Nick said.

But Tesla had already lost interest in the big contraption behind her. Now she was looking at the junk that she and her brother had taken cover behind.

"Hey," she said. "That's the stuff Uncle Newt said we could use to make a rocket."

Nick looked down. All he saw was a jumble of white plastic pipes, a manual air pump, a beat-up roll of duct tape, and a half-empty bottle of diet soda.

"Are you sure that's not the stuff that'll melt through the floor?" he said.

"Sure, I'm sure. Can't you see how we'd build the rocket?" Tesla challenged her brother with a cocked eyebrow.

Nick looked over the junk again. The adrenaline and fear were fading, and he was beginning to think clearly again.

A small, cautious smile tugged at the corner of his mouth. He still felt jumpy, on edge, but at least he knew a good way to distract himself.

"Of course, I see how to build it," he said. "Isn't it obvious?"

LOW-TECH (PRACTICALLY NO-TECH) BOTTLE ROCKET AND LAUNCHER

THE STUFF:

- 3 pieces of 10-inch (25.5-cm) PVC pipe (labeled ½ inch [1.25 cm] wide at hardware stores) (A)

- 3 pieces of 20-inch-long (51 cm) PVC pipe (B)

- 3 90-degree-angle pieces (C)

- 1 T connector (D)

- 2 end caps (E)

- 1 threaded end cap (F)

- 1 bicycle pump (G)

- 1 TR413 tire valve (can be acquired from an auto parts store or a garage that fixes tires) (H)

- 1 1- or 2-liter plastic soda bottle (I)

- Water

- Electrical tape

- PVC cement

- A drill

- Pliers

- Safety goggles

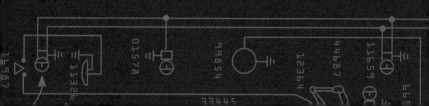

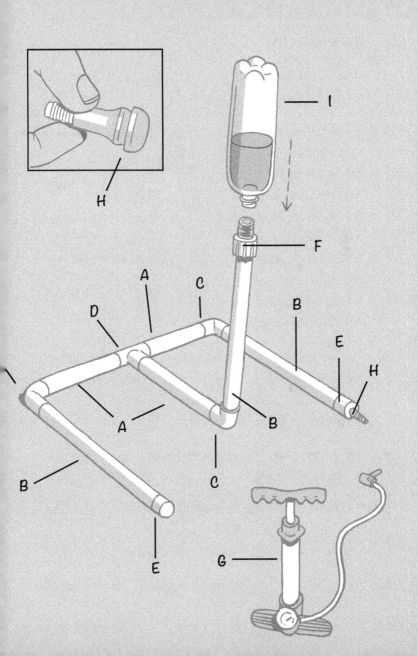

THE SETUP

1. Ask an adult to drill a ½-inch (1.25-cm) hole into the center of the flat side of one of the caps.

2. Feed the valve through the hole from the inside of the cap. Use the pliers to pull the valve through the hole so that the cap sits in the groove at the base of the valve. It may take a little twisting and tugging.

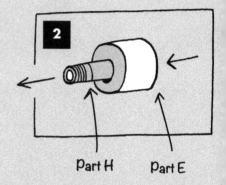

Part H   Part E

3. Gather the pipe, angle, and connector pieces together and lay them out as shown in the illustration. Working with an adult, follow the directions on the PVC cement to attach all the pieces snugly.

4. Let the completed launcher dry for as long as possible, preferably overnight.

5. The bottle goes over the vertical pipe in the middle. Wrap electrical tape around the threaded end cap until you get a tight fit when you place the neck of the bottle over it.

6. Go outside and make sure your launch area is clear of people and obstacles.

7. Fill the bottle one-third to halfway with water.

8. Turn the launcher upside down and twist the bottle snugly onto it.

9. Turn the launcher right side up and attach the bicycle pump securely to the valve.

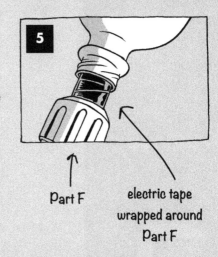

Part F

electric tape wrapped around Part F

THE FINAL STEPS

---

1. Put on your safety goggles and start pumping.

2. Be ready for the pressure to send the rocket flying!

3. If the rocket launches too soon (or doesn't go very high), add more electrical tape around the threaded end cap to create a tighter seal against the bottle.

WARNING: Never stand over an unlaunched rocket. If the rocket fails to launch after excessive pumping, it's possible the electric tape seal is too tight. Remove the pump from the tire valve. Then push the small pin inside the valve until all the air has been released (much as you would flatten a bicycle tire). Have an adult remove the bottle. Peel off three layers of electric tape from the launcher and give it another go.

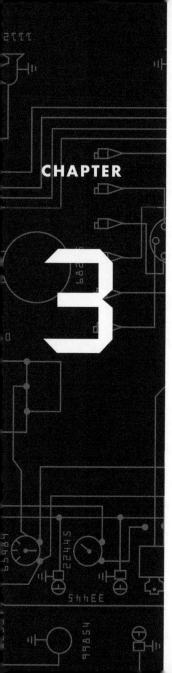

It took Nick and Tesla less than forty minutes to build the rocket. But Tesla insisted they take another ten minutes to search the basement (very, very warily, in Nick's case) for paint they could use to decorate it. Not long after they found some (in a cabinet marked MONKEY PROOF!!!, for some reason), the rocket was gleaming white with black panels and tips, classic NASA style. Tesla christened it with a name she painted on the nose cone in curly red letters: THE ALBERT AND MARTHA HOLT.

Albert and Martha Holt were

their parents.

"Dad always said he became a scientist because he wanted to ride on the space shuttle," Tesla said. "Well, now we can give him his ride. In spirit, anyway."

"How do you go from being a wannabe astronaut to being an expert on soybeans?" Nick asked.

"I don't know. We'll have to ask Dad."

"Yeah. The next time we talk to him . . . whenever that'll be."

"Hey, they said they'd call when they could. They're in Karakalpakstan, remember?"

Tesla was proud of herself for getting out *Karakalpakstan* on the first try.

Nick just nodded glumly.

Karakalpakstan was the region of Uzbekistan their parents were traveling to. Nick and Tesla had looked it up on Wikipedia. It was six times bigger than Texas and had one twenty-fifth as many people. Its one and only radio station had opened just a few months earlier.

Needless to say, there probably weren't many cell phone towers there.

Nick brought his hand up and touched his chest where the pendant their parents had given him made a little lump under his shirt. Tesla knew what he was thinking.

"We want you to wear these," Mom had told them as she hung the pendants around their necks. "So you'll always feel us with you, no matter how long we might be apart."

The next day, Nick and Tesla had been on a plane for California.

"Don't worry," Tesla told her brother, unconsciously bringing her fingers up to touch her pendant, too. "Mom and Dad'll be all right. Karakillpookstun—"

Tesla grimaced and tried again, enunciating carefully.

"*Karakalpakstan* isn't dangerous. It's just kind of . . . empty."

"Yeah. I'm sure you're right," Nick said.

But it didn't sound like he meant it.

While they waited for the cement and paint on the rocket launcher to dry, Nick and Tesla went looking for Uncle Newt. They found him in the same place he'd been the last time they'd looked for him: the master bathroom on the second floor. They'd dragged him out of the shower for help with the rocket—even Tesla, bold as she could be, knew better than to try her luck with a power drill—and he must've jumped right back in the second he could. It was understandable, actually. His hair had still been half orange.

The bathroom had what looked like a submarine airlock instead of a normal door, and unlike before it was now closed up tightly. When Nick and Tesla pressed their ears to the metal, they could dimly hear the sound of running water and Uncle Newt crooning "Winter Wonderland."

Outside, it was sunny and seventy degrees.

"Gone awaaaaaaay is the something! Here to staaaaaaaay is the something! We da-da-da daaaaaa, la-la-la la laaaaaaa! Something in a something booby baaaaaaaaa!"

"Uncle Newt!" Tesla yelled.

"Uncle Newt!" Nick yelled.

"Uncle Newt!" they yelled together.

"In the meadow we can something-something!" Uncle Newt sang. "And da-something something la-la-laaaaaa! We'll have something something with the something! Until the who-who ha-has jooby jaaaaaaaa!"

"Great," Nick sighed. "He's ignoring us now."

"I guess I can't blame him," said Tesla. "His hair was still half orange the last time we pulled him out of there."

"Well, I'm starving. Can we go see if the cat left us some cake?"

Tesla thought it over, weighing her hunger against the chance of eating cake a cat had licked.

She was very, very hungry.

"Good idea," she said.

Apparently, the cat had tired of icing after cleaning off a quarter of the cake. It was nowhere to be seen now, and Tesla guessed it had staggered off somewhere to sleep off its sugar buzz.

Already on the table were plates and forks and a knife, and Nick and Tesla served themselves slices of cake that were (they hoped) cat-spit free. Since there were no chairs in the room, only the strange straps dangling from the ceiling, they would have to eat standing up.

Nick put a forkful of cake in his mouth.

Tesla put a forkful in her mouth.

"Gah!" Nick said.

"Bleah!" said Tesla.

They spit the cake back onto their plates.

"Salt," said Nick.

Tesla nodded. "Instead of sugar."

She spat on her plate again.

Nick tossed his plate on the table and hurried toward the kitchen. "Ugh! I need something to drink!"

"Me, too," Tesla said, following her brother. "We'd better make it something from a can."

"Right."

Nick had tasted Uncle Newt's idea of cake. He had no desire to see what the man's homemade lemonade might be like.

"Hey! Chocolate milk!" Tesla said when they opened the refrigerator.

She started to take the plastic jug out of the fridge.

"Wait," Nick said.

He pointed at the expiration date stamped on the side. "February 22," it said.

"Whew," Tesla said as she put back the chocolate milk. "Close call."

Everything else in the refrigerator was just as old, with the mold to prove it. The only other liquid (other than some puddles of brown goo from rotten fruit) was a bottle of diet soda with MINE!!! written on the side and a specimen jar marked BYPRODUCT . . . ACID???

They found some glasses and got water from the tap.

"Tez, what would you call Uncle Newt?" Nick said. "A fruitcake or a flake?"

"Dad always called him 'eccentric' when he talked about him."

"And Mom would just roll her eyes."

"Well, Uncle Newt's not a fruitcake or a flake. He's . . . family."

"Yeah. Flakey, fruitcake family. Why do you think Mom and Dad sent us to stay with him instead of Grandma or Aunt Mary or the Harringtons? It's like they chose the least responsible, most checked-out, distant relative they could think of."

"Maybe they did."

"Why would they do that?"

"Change of pace?" Tesla said. She put her glass in the sink. "Come on. Let's go test our rocket."

The kids stepped out the back door onto Uncle Newt's tiny cracked-concrete patio. Nick carried the launcher and the pump. Tesla carried the rocket and a plastic jug filled with water. (The jug used to contain chunky chocolate milk sludge. It had been cleaned very, very thoroughly, but it still smelled like the bottom of a compost heap. Unfortunately, it was the only jug they could find that didn't have POISON or a skull and crossbones on it, so they were stuck with it.)

"Maybe not the best place for a launchpad," Nick said, looking out at the yard.

The grass was two feet high. Sprouting from it here and there were weeds as tall as Tesla.

"Front yard?" Nick said.

"Front yard," said Tesla.

They walked around the house and started setting up the launcher near the pole that the runaway lawn mower had been tethered to.

"Stop!" someone shrieked when they were almost done.

Nick and Tesla turned to find a woman standing at the edge of the neighboring yard. It was easy to see where the edge was. The grass on the woman's side was so immaculately manicured, it looked like a smooth green sheet.

"What do you think you're doing?" the woman snarled.

She was the woman Nick had seen earlier, the one who'd come back from the gym right after Uncle Newt's lawn mower chewed through her begonias.

She'd cleaned herself up and put on fresh clothes. But she was still scowling.

"We're—" Tesla began.

"No you are not!" the woman declared.

"We're just—" Tesla said.

"No, no, no!"

"We're just testing—"

"NO!"

Nick decided to see if he could get further than his sister.

"Excuse me," he said. He raised the rocket and tapped the tip. "This is just plastic and cardboard. It wouldn't hurt anything even if—"

"Oh, *sure*," the woman broke in. She crossed her arms over her chest and somehow managed to smirk without losing her scowl. "Your little missile is harmless."

"It's not a missile," Tesla said. "It's a rocket."

The woman didn't hear her. She never stopped talking long enough to try.

"Like the self-emptying garbage can that dumped twenty pounds of compost in my pool was harmless. Like the automatic car washer that scraped the paint off my Prius was harmless. Like the skunk trap that stunk up the neighborhood like a burning outhouse was harmless. That's a strange definition of *harmless* you people have!"

"Come on," Tesla muttered, picking up the launcher and the pump. "We'll find somewhere else to test the rocket."

She and Nick left Uncle Newt's yard and started up the street, although they had no idea where they were going. They were just heading in what was obviously the best direction: away from the woman.

"And tell your friend Dr. Frankenstein he owes me a garden gnome!" she shouted after them.

"He's our uncle!" Tesla called back over her shoulder.

The last thing they heard the woman say was, "My condolences!"

"At least he has a cool house," Nick said out of the blue.

He and Tesla had been wandering around the neighborhood for fifteen minutes looking for a park where they could test their rocket.

"Who? Uncle Newt?" said Tesla.

Nick nodded. "I'm counting silver linings. Like, I bet he won't make us pick up our rooms."

"Probably not."

"I bet he won't make us eat broccoli or brush our teeth."

"I bet not."

"I bet he won't give us chores. I bet he won't yell at us if we accidentally let the water in the bathtub overflow. I bet he won't ground us if one of our experiments blows up."

"I think you might be right."

Nick and Tesla walked a while in silence.

"I miss Mom and Dad," Nick said.

"Me, too," said Tesla.

They never did find a park. But they did find an empty field. It was at the northern edge of the neighborhood, where the road curved and became a private drive blocked by a black iron gate.

"Looks like Wayne Manor," Nick said, staring at the huge, run-down house the driveway led to.

"Or a haunted mansion," said Tesla. "I betcha a million bucks the local kids call it 'The Old Jones Place' or 'The Old Smith Place' or something like that."

"Deal," said Nick.

He and his sister made such bets all the time.

As Tesla figured it, Nick owed her fourteen million dollars.

"Come on," Tesla said.

She headed out into the field. It was lined on one side by a slim strip of trees. Just beyond, in the shade of their branches, was the tall fence that surrounded the Old Whoever Place. The field was big enough for a house and a yard, and not small ones, either. Yet, it was empty, a no-man's-land obviously meant to separate the estate from the rest of the neighborhood.

Whoever the Whoevers were, they sure liked their privacy.

The field was full of brittle yellow grass and reedy weeds. The soil felt loose and sandy. When Nick and Tesla were in the middle of the field, they could see why. The far end of the field sloped down to the bank of a narrow stream.

"We're pretty close to the ocean," Tesla said. "I bet that water flows right into it."

"Whoa!" Nick said.

The most interesting thing in their old neighborhood, he'd always thought, was their own house (and, more specifically, the projects and experiments he and Tesla were always tinkering with). The runner-up was a 7-Eleven. So, though Nick wasn't the most adventurous person in the world, having an ocean in the backyard sounded pretty cool.

"Maybe we could learn how to kayak," he said. "Or even surf!" He paused to ponder that idea, and his enthusiasm dimmed. "They have sharks around here, don't they?"

Tesla nodded. "Great whites."

Nick turned his back to the creek.

"That looks like a good spot to launch from," he said.

He walked to an especially smooth weed-free patch of ground nearby. Tesla followed, and soon they had their launcher ready. They both wanted to do the pumping, and neither wanted to pour the smelly water from the jug into the rocket. So they had to make a deal: Tesla would do the pouring, Nick would do the pumping. And Tesla would add another two million dollars to her brother's debt.

Tesla managed not to gag as she filled the rocket. When it was half full, Nick tipped over the launcher and screwed on the rocket. Then he straightened the launcher again, connected the pump to the pipes, and started forcing in air.

Tesla took a big step back. When the rocket launched, that nasty sour-milk water was going to spray everywhere.

"Is anything happening?" Nick asked.

Tesla took a cautious step forward. "I think I see some bubbles, but it's hard to tell."

"Oh, great. Good thing *someone* insisted on painting the bottle. Now we can't see what's going on inside."

"Shut up," Tesla said.

Nick started pumping up and down faster.

The rocket didn't move.

"Why isn't it working?" Nick said.

"I don't know."

Tesla started toward the rocket.

NICK AND TESLA'S HIGH-VOLTAGE DANGER LAB

Nick stopped pumping.

"I don't think you want to do that," he said.

"I just want to check the seal. Maybe it's not tight enough and air's leaking out."

Tesla bent down beside the launchpad.

"I *really* don't think you want to do that," Nick said.

Tesla ignored him.

As she leaned in to check the rocket, her pendant and chain draped over the nose cone. She didn't seem to notice. Nick did.

"Tesla!" he cried.

He reached toward his sister and accidentally knocked the pump handle down, providing the last puff of air the rocket needed. It shot upward with a high-pitched whiiiish, taking the pendant, the chain, and a small clump of Tesla's hair with it.

"Ow!" said Tesla. Then "Ew!" as the spray of foul-smelling water shooting out of the rocket drenched her head.

"No!" said Nick. "No, no, no!"

Despite the bungled launch, the rocket was flying faster and higher than they ever could have hoped. Which was the problem. Instead of going straight up and coming straight down, the bottle, weighted down

by its unintended cargo, was arcing to the right. As it plummeted to earth again, it was headed for the trees on the edge of the field.

Nick started running after it. "If it lands in the top branches we'll never get it down!"

"Don't freak out," Tesla grumbled. She took a quick test-sniff of her hair and grimaced. "It's not going fast enough to go as far as . . . oh."

The rocket zipped over the trees and landed with a little hollow *thud* on the wrong side of the tall fence surrounding the Old Whoever Place.

"Oh, no," Nick moaned as he trotted up to the fence. He put his hands on the crisscrossing wires and stared forlornly at the *Albert and Martha Holt*. "Should I climb over and get it?"

"Go for it," Tesla said. "And for the next launch, *you* get to pour the stink-water into the . . . Nick, look out!"

Two large dark shapes appeared on the other side of the fence and hurled themselves at Nick.

Nick yelped and yanked his hands away from the fence just in time. He jumped back, tripped over the nearest tree roots, and fell over backward.

"Are you all right?" Tesla said as she came running toward her brother.

Nick sat up and glared first at her and then at the two huge Rottweilers that stood between them and their rocket. The big black dogs were snarling and snapping and generally looking extremely disappointed that neither had managed to chomp off Nick's fingers.

"*Now* can I freak out?" Nick said.

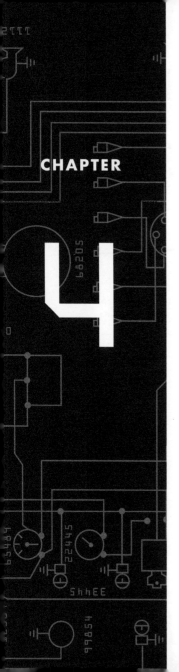

4

As Nick and Tesla walked along the fence toward the road, the dogs trotted along beside them, growling.

"It's not going to be a big deal," Tesla said in a way that told Nick she wasn't just trying to convince him; she was trying to convince herself, too. "I saw an intercom by the gate. We can just call the people in the house and ask them to get the rocket for us."

"Sure," Nick said. "It's not like the kind of people who'd live in a creepy old mansion with a fence around it and guard dogs the size of horses would mind if a couple strange kids decided to wander around their property. I'm sure they'll invite us in for milk and cookies."

Tesla rolled her eyes.

"Little Mr. Sunshine," she said.

Nick glared at her.

That was their mother's nickname for him.

When they got to the gate, Nick let his sister puzzle over the small rusty speaker and numbered keypad mounted on a low black pole.

"There should be a number here for calling the house," Tesla said. She tapped a narrow rectangular area along the bottom of the keypad, beneath all the buttons. It was slightly less faded and dusty than the rest of the intercom. "It looks like one used to be here, but someone took it off."

"Great," said Nick.

The dogs were pacing on the other side of the gate, still growling.

Nick growled back at them.

Tesla tried pushing random numbers. She tried pushing the star button. She tried pushing the pound button. She tried pushing both buttons at the same time. She tried pushing all the buttons at once.

"Hello? Hello? Hello? Hello? Hello?" she said.

Nothing happened.

"It's star one-nine-five," someone said.

Nick and Tesla turned around. Two boys on bikes were watching them from a few feet away. Nick had been so busy growling and Tesla so busy helloing that they hadn't even noticed the boys ride up.

"What?" Tesla said.

"To call the house," one of the boys said. He was tall and pudgy and had an unruly mop of thick black hair.

The other boy pointed at the intercom.

"They used to have it taped on there, I think, but it must have fallen off, like, a million years ago," he said. Physically, he was the opposite of his friend: small and wiry, with hair shaved so short he almost looked bald.

Both boys were wearing T-shirts and jeans. They looked like they were Nick and Tesla's age.

"So, how do you know the number?" Tesla asked.

The boys glanced at each other, grinning.

"When we saw the construction guys and their dogs, we started trying random numbers until someone came on and yelled at us to stop," said the big one.

"Construction guys?" said Nick.

"Yeah," said the smaller boy. "They showed up a few days ago. First time we'd seen anyone in the old Landrigan place in years."

Tesla shot her brother a smug look.

"The old Landrigan place, huh?" she said.

"Yeah, yeah," Nick muttered. "I owe you another million."

Tesla turned back to the boys.

"I'm Tesla, by the way. This is my brother, Nick."

"Hi. I'm DeMarco," said the smaller boy.

"I'm Silas," said the other. He took a sniff in Tesla's general direction. "Did someone dump sour milk on your head?"

Tesla clenched her jaw and flushed the color of cotton candy.

"No," she said. "I got sprayed by a water rocket."

"Huh?" said DeMarco.

"Chuh?" said Silas.

Tesla started telling them about the rocket and the pendant while Nick threw in the occasional dramatic flourish. ("And then those attack dogs came flying at me and nearly ripped my hands off!") Nick was usually pretty quiet around new people, but DeMarco and Silas were listening with such rapt attention, he couldn't resist.

"Well, good luck getting your rocket back," DeMarco said when Tesla was finished. His tone seemed to add, "You'll need it."

"Can we watch you call the house?" said Silas.

Tesla looked at him quizzically. "Uhh . . . all right. If you'd find that entertaining. What was the number again?"

DeMarco told her.

Tesla turned back to the keypad and punched the star button, then one and nine and five.

Once again, nothing happened.

Tesla glanced back at Silas and DeMarco. They were watching expectantly.

"Just give it a second," DeMarco said.

The intercom clicked, then buzzed in a low staticky way, like a bad telephone connection.

"Get away from that gate," a gruff voice snapped, "or I'm calling the cops."

"Excuse me? What?" Tesla said.

It wasn't that she hadn't understood the man. She was just surprised by his words.

"You heard me. We're working here. If you aren't gone in ten seconds, I'm dialing 911."

"Wait! We just want to get our rocket!" Tesla blurted out. "It flew over your fence, and there's something really important in the—"

"Tell your little fairy tale to the police."

There was another click, and the buzzing stopped.

The man had hung up.

The boys burst out laughing. It was obvious now why they'd wanted to watch.

"I'm sorry," DeMarco said when they were done guffawing. "It's just . . . that guy is such a jerk, it's hilarious!"

"Don't worry," said Silas. "He won't call the police. That's just something he likes to say."

"Well, I don't like hearing it," Tesla said.

Her chin jutted out in a way Nick knew well. She was gritting her teeth. Redoubling her resolve.

The universe was trying to tell her she'd never get the rocket—and, more important, the pendant their parents had given her—back again. But Nick had news for the universe. Something it should have already known.

Never tell Tesla Holt *never*.

"Who are these 'construction guys'?" she said.

"Oh, you know. Construction guys," Silas said. "They showed up with a work van and started . . . I don't know. Constructing, I guess."

"Renovating," DeMarco said.

"Right. That's it. They must be renovating. 'Cuz no one's lived in the old Landrigan place since, like, the Misozozoic."

"Mesozoic," Nick corrected.

Everyone ignored him.

"Not that all the Landrigans are gone," DeMarco said. He leaned forward over his handlebars, face solemn, eyebrows raised high. "Some say their spirits still roam the mansion, searching for their lost fortune. Maybe one has your rocket at this very moment."

Silas raised his hands and wriggled his fingers.

"Woooooooooo!" he said.

"Ghost stories are stupid," Tesla said.

Silas dropped his hands.

"Well, you're no fun," he said.

DeMarco started peddling his bike, doing a slow circle in the cul-de-sac.

"Come on," he said to Silas. "Let's go."

Silas started peddling, too, and a moment later the two boys were zipping off up the street.

"Bye!" Nick called after them. "See you later!"

"Bye," said Silas.

DeMarco gave a lazy one-handed wave, but he didn't look back or say anything.

"They seem all right," Nick said. "Maybe you shouldn't have called them stupid."

"I didn't say they were stupid. I said ghost stories are stupid." Tesla jutted out her chin. "And I *am* fun."

"Oh, yeah. I'm having the time of my life."

Tesla scowled at her brother.

"You want excitement?" she said. "I'll show you excitement."

She turned to face the Rottweilers that were still watching them from the other side of the gate, occasionally licking their big black chops.

"I'll be back," she said to them.

Then she pivoted on her heel and began striding up the street.

"Wait," Nick called after her. "Who said I wanted excitement? We were talking about *fun*."

Tesla didn't slow down.

Nick sighed, then hurried off after her.

Tesla banged on the bathroom airlock.

"Uncle Newt! I need to talk to you! Uncle Newt!"

Tesla paused in her pounding and brought her ear close to the metal door.

Nick leaned in beside her. He could hear running water and muffled, echo-y singing.

"It's beginning to look a lot like Christmas every place you stroll," Uncle Newt was warbling. "There's a dee in the da-da-da, a bee in the ba-ba-ba, and a something in the lee-lee la-la-laaaaaa!"

"I don't think he's coming out of there till it is Christmas," Nick said.

"Fine. We'll take care of ourselves," Tesla declared. "What we need is a distraction."

"You mean like TV?"

"Not for us," Tesla snapped. "For the dogs."

"Oh. So we're really going back?"

"You think I'm going to just give up the pendant Mom and Dad gave me?"

Nick pondered that a moment.

"The best distraction for a dog," he said, "would probably be food. Maybe we could use some from Uncle Newt's fridge somehow."

"You've looked in Uncle Newt's refrigerator. Do

you think there's anything in there even a dog would eat?"

Nick thought back to the four-month-old chocolate milk and the withered brown fruit so decayed it was impossible to tell if it had been oranges or apples.

"No," he said. "I guess not."

Tesla turned and started toward the stairs.

"Where are you going?" Nick asked.

"If we want a distraction, we're going to have to build one ourselves. And Uncle Newt did tell us we could 'go nuts' with his stuff. 'My laboratory is your laboratory,' remember?"

"Ahhh," Nick said.

He followed his sister down the steps.

When they got to the bottom of the staircase, they turned and headed toward their uncle's lab.

Their lab.

"Hey," Nick said as he and his sister poked through the scientific bric-a-brac (and just plain junk) in the basement, "maybe we could use Uncle Newt's spray-on clothes to give those dogs new orange muzzles."

"Nah," Tesla said. She picked up an opened roll of mints off a worktable, glanced at it, then put it back.

"They might suffocate."

"Oh. Well. I guess that would be sad," Nick said. "Kind of."

He was still mad at the guard dogs for almost giving him a heart attack.

Something on the floor in the corner caught Tesla's eye. She crouched down, reached a hand into the shadows and pulled out another half-empty soda bottle.

"Oh, man," Nick said. "If we'd found that before, we could've used it to carry the water, and your hair wouldn't smell like rancid cheese now."

Tesla shot her brother such a scowl he actually took a step back and bumped into something that had crept up behind him. He yelped in surprise.

Uncle Newt's bald cat darted around his ankles and ran up to Tesla. It must have followed them down the stairs.

"Now there's the perfect distraction for a couple dogs," Nick said.

He was grateful for a distraction himself—for his sister. As she scratched the cat's hairless head, she seemed to forget she should be mad at him. In fact, she looked up at him and grinned as if he'd just said something brilliant.

He thought back over his words—then opened his eyes wide and shook his finger at his sister.

"No way, Tez! We are *not* doing that to Uncle Newt's cat!"

Tesla gave the cat one last scratch, then stood up.

"Of course we're not," she said.

She picked up the mints again and started for the stairs.

"We're going to make our own cat," she said.

MINTS-AND-SODA-FUELED ROBOCAT DOG DISTRACTOR

THE STUFF:

- 1 2-liter bottle of diet cola
- 1 package of Mentos candies
- A paper clip
- A wire coat hanger
- A glue gun
- Scissors
- Paper
- A soup can
- 3 ballpoint pens

- Thick cardboard
- Wire cutters
- Pliers
- A nail
- A drill
- A pushpin
- A binder clip
- A responsible adult (to help with the drill and glue gun)

THE SETUP

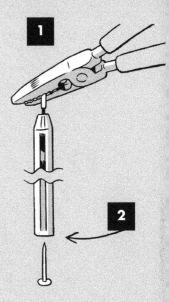

1. Use the pliers to pull the writing points and ink cartridges from two of the pens.

2. Use the nail to poke a hole through the other end of the pens. (If the ends are capped, you can simply remove the caps.)

3. Use the wire cutters to cut two straight pieces of coat hanger about 2 inches (5 cm) longer than the pens.

4. Put the soup can on the cardboard and trace four wheels. Use the scissors to cut out the wheels.

5. To find the exact center of each wheel, use the soup can to trace another circle on the piece of paper. Cut out the circle and fold it in half and then into quarters. When you unfold the paper circle, the creases will intersect in the middle. Place the paper circle over each cardboard circle and use the third pen—the one you haven't taken apart—to poke through the center.

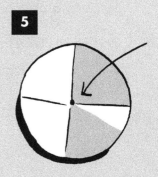

6. Using the pliers, bend one end of each coat hanger about ¾ inch (2 cm) from the end, forming a right angle.

7. Slide one of the wheels onto each wire and hot-glue the wheel in place. Make sure the wheels line up nicely with the wire, and be sure the glue doesn't get on the pen.

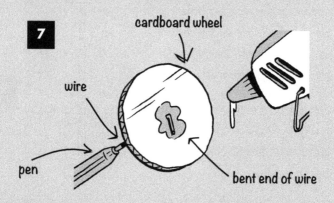

cardboard wheel

7

wire

pen

bent end of wire

8. Slide each wire through each of the empty pens and bend the non-wheel end of the wire.

9. Slide on another wheel and glue the wire to the wheel as in step 7, making sure the wheels line up. Once dry, the wheels should spin freely inside the pen.

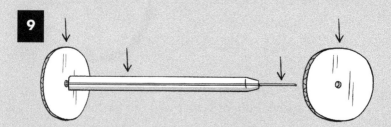

9

10. Hot-glue the pens onto the top and bottom of the soda bottle. Use plenty of glue to make sure they're secure, and check that the wheels line up correctly.

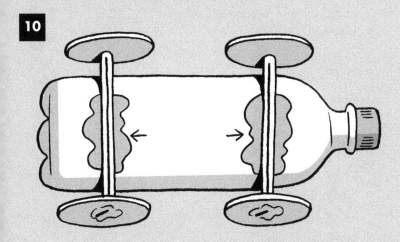

11. Have the responsible adult drill a ¼-inch (0.65-cm) hole in the middle of the soda cap.

12. Use the pushpin to *carefully* poke a hole through the middle of five Mentos candies, one at a time.

13. Straighten out the paper clip except for a small bend at one end. Poke the paper clip through each of the Mentos.

14. Place the cap on top of the Mentos by feeding the paper clip through the hole.

15. Use the binder clip to keep the paper clip from dropping through the cap.

THE FINAL STEPS

1. Determine a travel route
   and clear any obstacles
   out of the way. The rocket
   can travel up to 30 feet
   (9 m)—and once it starts,
   there's no turning back!

   15

2. Go to your testing loca-
   tion outside and securely
   screw the cap onto the
   bottle. *Be sure the Men-
   tos do not get soda on them.* You may need to pour out
   some of the soda.

3. Remove the binder clip, allowing the Mentos to drop into
   the soda.

4. Quickly tilt the rocket car onto its wheels.

5. Stand back! When the mints are submerged in the soda,
   they produce plenty of extra carbon dioxide. This exploding gas is what turns a plastic bottle into a whizzing
   rocket car.

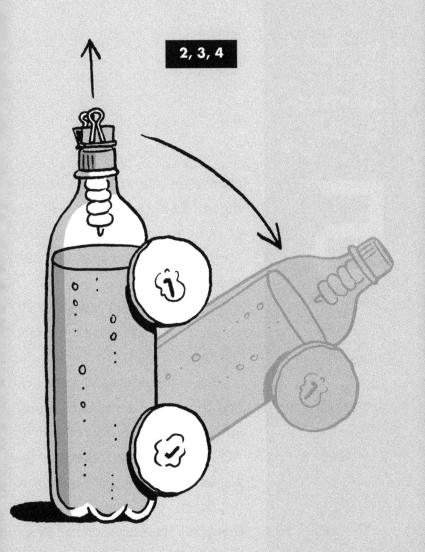

2, 3, 4

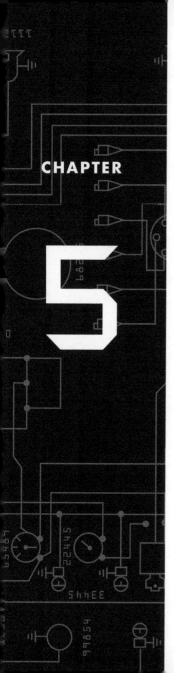

5

Nick won the coin toss. Which meant he'd *lost*, really. But he couldn't complain. There wouldn't have been a coin toss at all if he hadn't insisted on one.

"Okay," Tesla said grimly. "You'll go over the fence, and I'll distract the dogs."

She'd wanted to climb the fence and get the pendant back herself, but Nick had insisted they flip for it. After all, it was *their* rocket and the pendant had been a gift—maybe an important one, somehow—from their parents. And Nick had been the one who'd nudged the pump and sent the rocket flying. So why should Tesla automatically take the big risk?

Nick could think of a good answer for that question, actually: because he wouldn't have nudged the pump in the first place if his sister hadn't gotten too close to the launcher. But it was too late now. He had to go and be all noble. Idiot.

"You sure you really want to do this?" Tesla asked.

"Absolutely," Nick lied.

Tesla looked dubious, but she didn't call him on it.

They were crouched down in the field by the Old Landrigan Place, and they both turned toward the fence and looked for the guard dogs. The animals were nowhere in sight.

"Probably off sharpening their fangs," Nick said. It would have gone over better as a manly, laugh-in-the-face-of-danger joke if his voice hadn't been quavering so badly.

"Well, don't worry about that," Tesla said. "Remember, we brought something for them to sink their fangs into."

She picked up RoboCat. She and Nick had added a crude cardboard head and paws to the soda bottle to make it look more catty. Now that the glue and paint were dry (as well as Tesla's hair, which she'd been forced to wash in the sink because her uncle was still hogging the bathroom), it was ready. But were they?

"I'll make noise till I've got the dogs' attention," she said. "Then I'll let RoboCat go. Once they take off after it, I'll whistle. That'll be your signal to climb the fence and find the rocket and the pendant. They should be right on the other side of that rose bush over there. You'll probably have plenty of time."

It bothered Nick that she didn't say "You *will* have plenty of time," but he tried not to let his distress show.

He gave his sister what he hoped was a jaunty salute.

She stood and started toward the gate to the estate's private drive. As she got close, Nick began moving toward the fence in a creeping crouch. He had to be ready to act fast when the moment came. But if the guard dogs spotted him too early, it was all over. They'd be so obsessed with the nice, juicy, delicious-looking kid that they'd never stop barking and drooling long enough to notice RoboCat. So Nick stayed low.

About ten yards from the fence, he froze. One of the dogs had come padding around the house. The tongue that hung from the side of its mouth was so big and floppy it looked like a fat pink necktie.

The dog scanned the horizon, looking for something to kill.

"Yoo hoo!" Nick heard Tesla call out. "Defenseless child here! Come and get it!"

The dog started barking, and instantly its twin came flying around the house to join it. Together, they charged off toward the gate.

Tesla whistled, though it must have been obvious she didn't have to. A plan's a plan. You stick to it.

Nick ran to the fence and started climbing. When he reached the top, he paused to see if he'd been spotted.

The dogs were moving away from him, tearing up the looping driveway in pursuit of a brown shape zipping along low to the ground, a geyser of foam shooting out behind it.

RoboCat was working! For maybe another six seconds, anyway. As soon as the dogs caught it—and they were gaining fast—it was history.

Nick swung himself over the fence, climbed down a few feet, and then dropped the rest of the way. The second he had his feet on the ground, he turned and scurried around the rose bush and . . .

... started calling himself names.

"Ooo, you moron! You dummy!"

Nick had been so concerned about the dogs, he hadn't asked a key question.

What if the rocket and pendant aren't there?

They weren't.

Off in the distance, Nick could hear the dogs snarling and snapping. It sounded as though they were fighting each other, which would make sense if they'd just caught something worth fighting over.

RoboCat was toast. If Nick didn't move fast, then

he would be, too.

He looked all around the rose bush and the lawn, but there was no sign of the rocket or the pendant. He did catch a glimpse of his sister, though. She was still standing by the gate, watching him with an expression that was equal parts anger and horror. She flapped her hands toward the fence frantically, motioning for him to GO, GO, GO! But Nick could still hear the dogs fighting over the scraps of poor RoboCat somewhere around the corner of the house, and he decided he wasn't going to leave just yet. Why give himself a heart attack and have nothing to show for it?

He turned and skulked off, keeping close to the fence and the trees that loomed up over it. The dogs had come from the back of the house. Maybe that's where they'd taken the rocket. If Nick was lucky, he'd find it there. And if he was very lucky, the pendant would still be attached instead of making its way through a Rottweiler's intestinal tract.

When Nick could see around the house into the backyard, he finally appreciated just how rich the Landrigans (whoever they were) had been. They didn't just have a huge house all for themselves. They had another large one for all their cars in the form of a two-story garage at the end of the driveway.

A dog barked and Nick went still, his skin tingling. But the bark was muffled and distant. And it was more high-pitched than the Rottweilers' deep, guttural *rowff*! Nick couldn't be sure, but it sounded like it was coming from inside the garage.

He took a step toward the backyard and then froze again. He wasn't a believer in ESP—there was no scientific proof of it, his parents always pointed out—yet he was suddenly struck by a feeling so strong, it was almost like a voice speaking to him out of nowhere.

You're being watched, it said.

Nick looked to the left, to the right, and then finally up—and there she was.

A young girl in a nightgown was gazing down at him from a second-floor window. She had pale skin and long black hair and circles under dark, sunken eyes that bored into him with an intensity that made him shiver. It was a look of both infinite sadness and panic, as if the girl had been waiting and watching for Nick forever but, now that he was finally there, found him horrifying.

Nick gave the girl a hesitant little wave. You don't want to be rude when a ghost's staring at you.

The girl ducked away from the window. A moment later, she returned clutching a large notepad. She scribbled on it quickly, then held the pad up to the glass to show what she'd written.

GO AWAY!!!
 !!!

Nick was still blinking up at the girl's message when he realized the Rottweilers were barking again—and the barking was getting louder. As in,

closer. As was another sound.

Nick turned and saw a white van passing through the gate and starting up the driveway, the barking dogs running alongside. A ladder was secured to the top of the van, and Nick could see words printed on the side in big black letters: SIRINGO BROS. HOME RENOVATORS.

Instead of heading to the front of the house, the van was coming around the back. Toward Nick.

The dogs would see him any second.

🙁, indeed.

Nick whirled around and sprinted for the fence. He'd just gotten his hands on it when he heard the dogs' barks change, shifting in an instant from a yapping greeting/warning to a feral "You're dead!" snarl.

They'd spotted him, and Nick climbed accordingly. Fast and frightened.

Just as he got one leg over the top, he felt a hard jerk on the other, and he nearly lost his balance.

Nick looked down and saw one hundred twenty pounds of slobbering dog attached by the teeth to the bottom of his jeans.

Before he could even scream, something else grabbed his hand.

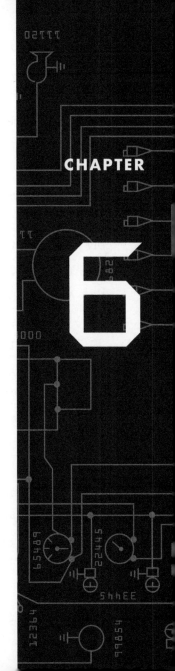

6

Nick fell.

Onto his sister, fortunately. Not that it was so fortunate for her.

When Tesla jerked her brother out of the dog's jaws, he rolled over the top of the fence and crashed down on top of her, laying her out flat on her back on the hard, dry ground.

"Oof!" said Tesla and Nick.

"Kill, kill, kill, kill, kill!" said the Rottweilers. Not in English, of course. They just pressed their big black snouts up close to the fence and kept barking furiously.

"Jaws! Claws!" a man called out.

"What ya got over there?"

"*Hide*," Tesla whispered.

Nick was already scrambling behind a tree trunk.

Tesla flipped over and crawled behind the next tree over.

"Quiet!" the man roared.

The dogs went from barking to whimpering.

"I don't see anything," another man said. "Probably just a squirrel."

"Yeah," the first man said. He sounded like the jerk who'd threatened to call the cops on them. "Maybe."

There was a moment of silence, then the sound of footsteps.

The men were walking away.

"Jaws! Claws! Come!"

The dogs growled and then trotted off after their master.

Still, Nick and Tesla waited a long, long time before they risked peeks around their respective trees.

"That was close," said Nick.

"That was *crazy*," said Tesla. "What took you so long? And where's the rocket? And the pendant?"

"Duh, Tez. You just answered your own questions.

What took me so long was I couldn't find the rocket or the pendant. Oh! And something else!"

Nick craned his neck, trying to get a look at the window the girl had been standing in. But it was around the corner of the house. You had to be on the estate grounds to see it.

"I saw someone in the house. A girl," Nick said. "A way-spooky girl."

Tesla cocked her head and shot her brother a disdainful look.

"Not funny," she said.

"Not joking!" said Nick. "She even told me to go away."

"She talked to you?"

"No. She made a sign and held it up in the window. 'Go away.' With a frowny face."

Tesla scoffed. "Oh, yeah—that is spooky. A frowny face? Terrifying!"

"I guess you had to be there."

"Why would a creepy little girl be in the house with the renovation guys, anyway? What is it, Take Your Ghost to Work Day?"

"Hey, I'm just telling you what I saw."

"Yeah." Tesla scanned the estate as best she could

from behind her tree. "And what you didn't see."

Nick looked, too.

"Your pendant must still be over there somewhere," he said. "Assuming the dogs didn't eat it."

"Even if they did eat it, we could still get it back."

"What do you mean?" Nick asked.

The answer dawned on him before his sister could say a word.

"Ewwwwwwwwwwww!"

"Let's just hope it doesn't come to that," Tesla said. She stood and walked off toward their homemade launchpad.

"Where are you going?" Nick asked.

"Back to the drawing board," Tesla told him.

A moment later, she picked up the launcher and the air pump and started toward Uncle Newt's house.

When they got to the house, they found Uncle Newt hanging from the ceiling.

"Hey, kids!" he said. "Have some 'za!"

He was dangling from the straps in the dining room, suspended horizontally about a foot above the table.

Nick was starving, but he didn't forget to look before he leaped (or ate). He smiled in a feeble, cautious way and pointed at the slice of pizza in Uncle Newt's hand.

"Did you make that yourself?" he asked.

"Me? No. I don't know if you could tell from the cake, but I'm not much of a cook. The pizza's from a place up the road. It's on the counter in the kitchen."

Nick and Tesla smiled at each other in relief, then rushed into the kitchen.

"Could you bring me some more?" Uncle Newt called after them. "Once I strap myself in, it's kind of a pain to get down."

"Why do you eat like this, anyway?" Tesla asked a minute later as she handed her uncle a slice of anchovy pizza. (Both she and her brother hated anchovies. Fortunately, half the pizza was plain. Uncle Newt was one of the most irresponsible adults Nick and Tesla had ever met, but at least he knew that not everyone likes pizza covered in slimy, oversalted strips of fish.)

"There are three reasons," Uncle Newt said. He took a huge bite of pizza and chewed on it happily, which didn't stop him from talking. "First, a hypothesis. Our ape ancestors didn't sit on chairs and they didn't use forks and knives to eat. They ate with their hands, and they were hanging from branches while they did it. Therefore, I submit to you that the human digestive tract should work most efficiently when the body is flat and off the ground."

"Shouldn't we be eating raw fruit, then?" Nick asked. "It's not like our 'ape ancestors' had Pizza Hut."

"Good point," Uncle Newt said.

Tesla jabbed a bony elbow into Nick's side.

"What?" he said.

Tesla just glared at him.

If their uncle threw out the pizza and made them eat bananas for dinner, she was going to kill him.

"Unfortunately," Uncle Newt said, "I can't stand raw fruit. Now, second reason: When my brother (your father) and I were young, we used to dream of being astronauts."

"We know," Tesla said.

"Well, we grew so obsessed with the idea that we tried to add these to our house." Uncle Newt waved his pizza at the thick gray straps he was hanging from. "You know. So we could eat in a simulated zero-g environment."

"Oh, sure," Nick said nonchalantly, as if all kids dreamed of stringing themselves up like piñatas and eating three feet off the ground.

"Of course, because we were seven and five at the time, we didn't do the best job of it," Uncle Newt said. "Brought down half the dining room ceiling, in fact. We were grounded until we were eight and six. But I vowed that when I was a grown-up with my own house, I'd give it another shot. So I did. Your dad never talked about trying it in your house?"

Nick and Tesla shook their heads.

Uncle Newt stared off into space with a wistful look. "That's too bad."

"What was the third reason?" Tesla asked.

"The what?"

"The third reason you hang yourself from the ceiling to eat."

"Oh. Right." Uncle Newt narrowed his eyes, then shrugged. "You know, I can never remember that one. Hey, did you end up building a rocket?"

"Yeah," said Nick.

"Did it work?"

"Too well. Do you know the Landrigan place?"

said Tesla.

"Sure. Everything around here used to be the Landrigan place."

"What do you mean?" Nick asked.

"All the land this neighborhood's built on used to be part of the Landrigan estate. They were reclusive people, apparently. A little, you know . . ."

Uncle Newt whistled and circled a finger around one ear.

"Not normal, like us," Nick said.

Uncle Newt nodded. "Exactly. Eventually, they started to have money problems. Sank most of their cash into a chain of disco bowling alleys. Or was it ostrich farming? Anyway, some kind of investment went belly-up. They had to start selling off their land piece by piece until all that was left was the mansion. I think the last Landrigan died there maybe ten years ago."

"Have you ever heard about any Landrigans . . . uh, you know . . . coming back?" Nick asked.

"To live in the mansion?"

Nick shrugged. "Or whatever."

Tesla rolled her eyes.

"No, I haven't heard about anything like that,"

Uncle Newt said. "But then again, I'm not the guy to come to for local gossip. I don't socialize much with the neighbors. A lot of strange uptight folks, if you ask me. The only person around here I talk to on a regular basis is Julie Casserly next door, and that's just because she's the weirdest, loudest one of the bunch. Always worked up about some ridiculous thing or other."

"Oh. That reminds me," Tesla said. "I think we met Julie. She says you owe her a garden gnome."

"A garden gnome?" Uncle Newt shook his head and laughed. "See? What'd I tell you? Kooks!"

With a loud *meow*, the hairless cat sauntered into the room, jumped up on the table, and started licking what was left of the icing off the cake.

"Down, Eureka!" Uncle Newt said. "Stop that!"

He tried to push the cat off the table, but it stayed just out of his reach even when he started swinging himself back and forth in his harness.

"Down! Shoo! That's for the kids! Go! Get!"

The cat just turned its back to him and kept eating.

Nick and Tesla looked at each other and sighed in unison.

Their uncle wasn't going to be any help getting Tesla's pendant back, and the only other grown-up they knew in town—in the entire *state*—was a neighbor-lady who already seemed to hate them.

Nick and Tesla chewed their pizza in silence, trying to enjoy something good while they could.

The first day of their summer "vacation" was drawing to a close, and it had been . . . eventful.

And kind of a disaster.

After dinner, Uncle Newt unstrapped himself and announced that he was headed to his laboratory to "toy with a few new notions" that had come to him as he ate. It would be tricky work, he said, and he'd need privacy. Nick and Tesla were welcome to look through his books or play games ("There might be a Parcheesi board around here somewhere") or do whatever modern kids did to amuse themselves.

"Have fun!"

And Uncle Newt disappeared into the basement.

Nick and Tesla were too exhausted and overwhelmed and bummed out to do anything but watch

TV. But even at that, they didn't last long. The television was powered by converted kinetic energy—either Nick or Tesla had to be jumping, hard, on the trampoline connected to it or it wouldn't stay on.

After the day they'd had, neither felt like jumping for joy. Or for an old PBS science show about black holes, which was the only interesting thing on, anyway.

They went to the stairs leading to the lab and called down to Uncle Newt that they were ready for bed.

"Wha'?" they heard their uncle say, and then there was a crash and a flash of light.

A puff of smoke that smelled like burnt marshmallows came rolling up the staircase.

"Are you all right?" Nick said.

There was a moment of eerie silence, then a cough, then a quiet "I'll be right there."

When Uncle Newt appeared at the top of the stairs a moment later, he looked slightly singed. But he was smiling.

"Sleep tight! Don't let the bedbugs fight!"

"Uhh . . . we won't," Nick said.

Uncle Newt turned to go.

"Oh," he said, stopping in the doorway. "I should probably warn you. Your beds might take a little getting used to."

"Why?" Tesla asked. "What's wrong with them?"

When Uncle Newt had shown them their room earlier, the beds had looked normal enough. Not that Nick and Tesla had paid much attention to them. They'd been distracted—and horrified—by the posters haphazardly stapled to the wall: Teletubbies, Elmo, Smurfs, Albert Einstein, and the periodic table. (Nick and Tesla had quickly agreed that the first three would "fall down" and "accidentally" "get ripped" at the first opportunity.)

"There's nothing wrong with your beds, and everything right!" Uncle Newt declared. "I'm telling you, kids. You haven't slept till you've slept on compost!"

"What?" Nick and Tesla said together.

Even Uncle Newt couldn't miss the disgust on their faces.

"Maybe I'd better come up and explain," he said.

Uncle Newt pulled the comforter off Nick's bed and revealed something that didn't look like a bed at all. It was more like a lumpy black sleeping bag with tubes and wires poking out of one end.

"Behold!" Uncle Newt said. "The biomass thermal conversion station!"

Nick reluctantly gave it a test-sit. It felt like he was lowering himself onto a garbage bag stuffed with rotten old food.

Because he was.

"As you sleep," Uncle Newt explained, "your body heat will help decompose food scraps pumped into the unit, which will in turn produce more heat that the convertor will turn into electricity. So, by the time you wake up in the morning, you'll have enough power to—ta da!"

Uncle Newt waved his hands at a coffeemaker sitting on the floor nearby.

"Brew coffee?" Tesla said.

Uncle Newt gave her a gleeful nod.

"We don't drink coffee," said Nick.

"Then you can have a hot cup of invigorating fresh-brewed water."

"Great," Nick said. He experimented with a little

bounce on his "bed." He could feel slimy things squishing and squashing beneath his butt.

"Comfy?" Uncle Newt asked.

"Uhh . . . kind of," Nick said.

Uncle Newt beamed at his invention.

"Patent pending," he said.

Uncle Newt was a gangly man with graying hair, but at that moment he looked like a five-year-old thinking about Christmas.

Tesla gave the room a tentative sniff. "Shouldn't the compost stink?"

"Oh, no, no, no, no, no! Each biomass thermal conversion station is completely airtight!" Uncle Newt's smile wavered just the teeniest bit. "In theory."

Nick opened his mouth to ask another question, but Uncle Newt didn't seem to notice.

"Well," he said, slapping his hands together, "I guess you two should wash your teeth and brush your faces and all that. Good night!"

And he went striding out the door.

"Good night," Nick said glumly.

Tesla was slowly lowering herself onto the big bag of putrid food she was expected to sleep on. From her expression, Nick thought there was a good chance she'd be spending the night on the floor. He saw her reach up reflexively to toy with something hanging around her neck. Something that wasn't there anymore.

"Good night?" Tesla said. "Yeah, right."

Nick read for a while. Tesla stared up at Albert Einstein.

After the third time he found himself falling asleep midsentence, Nick put down his book.

"We're going to go back for the pendant again tomorrow, aren't we?" he said.

"Of course we are. That pendant isn't just important to me. You said it yourself: It's important-important, somehow."

Nick nodded. "Fine. I just wanted to know what kind of nightmares to have tonight. See ya in the morning."

"See ya."

Nick turned out the light and closed his eyes.

When sleep came over him again, he expected to drift into visions of black fur and hateful hungry eyes, snapping jaws, and big sharp claws. But his mind stuck on a different image: a pale frightened-looking girl holding up a sign that said Go Away.

As Nick's sleep deepened and dreams took hold, the girl's scared face shifted, morphed. The cheeks rounded, the mouth bent, the eyes retracted into lifeless dots.

The girl became a cartoon. Or maybe more like something on a signpost. A hint about what lay ahead.

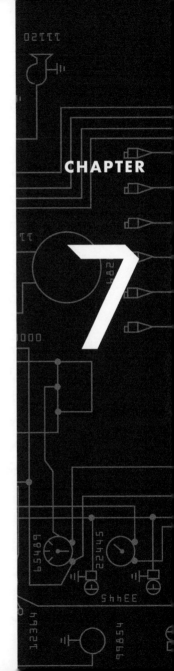

"I've been thinking," Tesla said when she saw her brother stir.

Nick blinked. The room was bathed in gray light. The coffeemaker was gurgling as hot, clear water filtered down into the pot.

It was morning.

"You're always thinking," Nick croaked.

"I've been thinking about that girl you saw."

"Yeah?"

That was the best Nick could manage before his first cup of steaming water.

"Yeah," Tesla said. "I was thinking about how to look for my pendant, but then I got stuck on the girl."

Nick thought back to the dreams he'd had that night.

"I know the feeling," he almost said but stopped himself just in time.

He knew how his sister would tease him if he said something like *that*.

"Yeah?" he said again.

"Yeah. You really saw her, right? It wasn't just a bad joke or a cloud reflected in the window?"

"No! I really saw her!"

"Okay, okay! It's just a little weird, don't you think? Like, why is a kid there while the house is being restored? And why would she bother writing 'Go away'? If she'd really wanted you gone for some reason, she could have told that nasty renovator guy about you. Or she could have just ignored you and let you become Dog Chow. But instead she wrote you a message."

Nick nodded thoughtfully. "You're right. It doesn't make sense. And looking at her . . . I don't know. Even from a distance, I could tell something was off. Wrong. She looked really unhappy."

"Hmm," Tesla said.

"Yeah," said Nick. "Hmm."

"I think when we go back for the pendant, I'm going to have a little talk with that girl."

"How are you going to manage that?"

"I've got an idea. But we'll need another RoboCat."

"I figured we would. And I have an idea for improving *that*."

"Great. Should we get to it?"

"First things first," Nick said. He put his hands on his stomach, which gurgled and growled as he stood up. "I *really* hope there's leftover pizza."

There was a note on the dining room table when Nick and Tesla came downstairs.

OUT FOR SUPPLIES!
BACK BY ~~LUNCH~~ DINNER!
—Uncle N. PROBABLY!

The pizza box was in the fridge. Empty.

Nick and Tesla split stale crackers and an ancient can of pork and beans for breakfast.

"Is this child abuse?" Nick asked as they ate.

"It will be if we have to eat this way again for dinner," Tesla said.

The only other edible food they'd found was a can of creamed corn.

"At least Uncle Newt went to the store," said Nick.

"Yeah. But what if he comes back with twenty more cans of creamed corn?"

Nick thought it over.

"You wanna run away?" he asked.

"Not quite yet," Tesla said. "We've still got things to do."

She started toward the stairs to the lab.

An hour later, Nick and Tesla were on their way to the old Landrigan place. Tesla was wearing a pink backpack she'd found in the closet of their room. She guessed it had been meant as a Christmas or birthday present for her several years before, for it still had a price tag attached and a cartoon kitten on the back under the words AIN'T I JUST THE CUTEST?

So, there was one advantage to being exiled thousands of miles from your home for the summer: You could walk down the street wearing a kindergartener's kitty-cat backpack and not worry about your friends coming out and laughing at you.

Nick, meanwhile, was carrying RoboCat II, a.k.a. RoboSquirrel. It was pretty much identical to the original RoboCat except it had a bushier tail (a feather duster Nick had found inexplicably mixed in with a box of duck decoys and what looked like dynamite). Nick had wanted to build two RoboSquirrels and coat them with smooshed slices of Uncle Newt's welcome cake. (One plain RoboThing hadn't distracted Jaws and Claws long enough, in his educated opinion.) But they could find only one more soda bottle for power, and even voracious attack dogs would probably turn up their noses at Uncle Newt's cake, especially when mint-flavored Diet Coke was spraying everywhere already. And anyway, Tesla said she'd be in and out in half the time her brother had taken.

"Wait," Nick said. "How are you going to do that and talk to the girl? And why should you be the one taking the risk this time?"

"I'll explain when we get there."

After they'd crossed the field and crept through the trees and watched for the dogs a while, Nick said, "All right, the coast is clear. Now tell me why you should go in with those dogs and not me?"

"It's like this," Tesla said, and she darted to the fence and started climbing as quickly (yet quietly) as she could.

"Hey!" Nick said.

Tesla slowed down just long enough to glance back and shush him. A few seconds later, she was dropping down to the ground on the other side of the fence.

"Well, what are you waiting for?" she whispered to her brother. "Get down to the gate and give those guard dogs something to chase."

"Fine. I'm going," Nick said sullenly. He started to leave but then suddenly stopped. "Just . . . don't get eaten, all right?"

"Deal," said Tesla.

Nick hurried off toward the road.

Tesla turned and headed in the opposite direction, toward the backyard. She stuck close to the fence, where she'd be shrouded (she hoped) in the shadows of the trees. She scanned the yard for their rocket, though a part of her—the pessimistic side that she (unlike her brother) rarely listened to—said she wouldn't see it. The grass was tall and thick, almost reaching her knees. It looked like it hadn't been mowed in . . . well, ever. Whoever had brought in the construction guys to fix up the house would need a whole other crew just to de-jungle the lawn.

Eventually, Tesla could see around the house to the backyard. It sloped down past the big freestanding garage her brother had mentioned. The construction guys' van was parked nearby.

Tesla watched the van for a moment, just in case one of the Siringo borthers was in back getting a power saw or a hammer or a ham sandwich.

Oooooo—ham sandwich, Tesla's stomach growled.

"Shut up," she told it.

She started moving closer to the house, listening intently for the sound of barking or panting or giant paws pounding the ground. When she was underneath the window Nick had told her about—second floor, farthest over on the right—she dug a hand into her pants pocket and pulled out her first batch of

Clandestine Communications Facilitators. The ones she'd collected on the way over.

Pebbles.

She started tossing them, one by one, at the window. Her first few attempts bounced off the house's grungy peeling siding. Soon, though, she got the range right, and she was getting a satisfying little *plink* with every throw.

Of course, Tesla knew that the girl might not be in the room again. Or she might be painting a wall while wearing earbuds with her iPod cranked up. Or she might be running down the hall screaming, "Release the hounds!" Or—

A girl appeared in the window. She was just as Nick had described her. Pale, slight, dark haired, sad. And surprised.

Tesla smiled and held up a finger. Then she whipped off her backpack and pulled out her second Clandestine Communications Facilitators: a legal pad and a black marker. The first message was already written on the top page.

"HI! I'M TESLA! WHO ARE YOU?"

The girl furrowed her brow and then stepped away from the window. Tesla assumed she knew where she'd gone and took the opportunity to steal a quick look around. No dogs, no irate construction dudes, no cops.

When she looked back up, Tesla saw what she'd expected: the girl holding up her own message.

"GO AWAY!!!"

No frowny face this time, but three exclamation marks. She meant it.

Tesla just held up her pad again and pointed at three words in quick succession.

WHO
ARE
YOU?

The girl pointed emphatically at the paper in her hand, stabbing at certain words just as Tesla had.

GO
AWAY!!!

Tesla was ready for that, too. She flipped to the next page, and her next message.

WHY?

The girl took down her notebook, wrote in it frantically, then pressed it against the glass again.

"MR. SNUGG," she'd written on it.

Tesla was jotting down her reply—"WHO?"—when she heard barking behind her. It was muffled, though, and she couldn't see any dogs.

What she did see was a burly man in jeans and a plaid shirt and blue windbreaker coming out the back door of the house and walking toward the van. It was sheer luck he hadn't noticed her—and there was no way that luck would last.

Tesla darted around the corner and ran for the fence, thinking she'd hide a while and then go back to continue her conversation with the girl. But as she crossed the driveway, she heard more barking off to her left—the deep, growly yapping of Jaws and Claws—and then a man shouted, "Hey!"

Time to go.

Tesla jammed the legal pad and marker into the world's most embarrassing backpack, strapped it on again, and scrambled up and over the fence. Once she'd dropped safely to the ground on the other side, she breathed a sigh of relief and started toward the road. She thought she'd meet her brother by the front gate and the two of them could figure out their next move.

Instead, Nick met her after she'd barely taken a step. He came charging through the trees, a look of panic on his face.

"Tesla!" he said.

That was all he got out before the man behind him—the man who'd been *chasing* him—snagged him by the back of the shirt and dragged him to a halt.

"Perfect," the man sneered when he saw Tesla. "Now I've got both of you!"

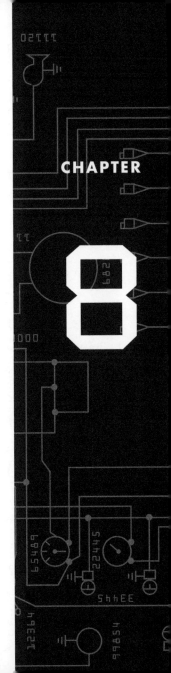

8

Nick struggled to free himself from the man's grasp.

The man gave him a shove that sent him slamming into the ground.

"Hey!" Tesla said, rushing to bend down beside her brother.

The man crossed his arms over his chest and scowled down at them. His head was shaved completely bald, and he was wearing a tight black T-shirt and black jeans. He wasn't especially tall or brawny, but there was something unsettlingly imposing about the way he just stood there. He seemed immovable, impassable, like a human version of the fence that pinned them in on one side.

"You all right?" Tesla asked Nick.

He nodded, but he looked shaken.

Tesla helped him up and then turned on the man.

"What's your problem?" she demanded. "Why are you running around terrorizing a helpless little kid?"

"'Helpless little kid'?" Nick said. He was scared, yet he managed to look offended, too.

"Why have *you* been sneaking around spying?" the man snapped at Tesla. His voice sounded familiar.

"Spying?" Tesla said. "We weren't spying. We were looking for a rocket we built. It landed in the Landrigans' yard yesterday, and when we came to ask for help getting it back, you just yelled at us."

The man cocked his head ever so slightly but didn't contradict her.

Obviously, she'd guessed right: This was the jerk they'd spoken to over the intercom the day before.

"You were trying to get your toy back," he said skeptically, "by feeding my dogs fake squirrels and soda?"

"*Your* dogs?" Tesla was about to shoot back. "Why do you need those monsters when you're doing home renovations?"

114

Hey, she thought. *That's actually a* really *good question.*

Nick spoke before she could.

"The fake squirrel was just a distraction," he said. "So the dogs wouldn't be howling at us while we looked for the rocket."

As if on cue, Jaws and Claws came trotting up on the other side of the fence. They sat at attention as close as they could get, their noses practically pressed up against the wires. They stared unblinkingly at the man, waiting for orders from the alpha of the pack.

Another man walked up behind them with the same sort of look on his face. It was the big muscular guy Tesla had seen walking out to the van. It looked like he hadn't shaved in a week.

"Need any help, Vince?" he said.

The bald man squinted at the kids while he mulled it over.

"Yeah," he finally said, glancing this way and that. "Maybe you should come around here and . . ."

Something he saw off toward the road froze him for a second.

"On second thought, Frank, I'm gonna be nice."

He turned back to Nick and Tesla. "I'll let you two off with another warning. Your *last*, you understand? This is private property. Trespassers will be dealt with. Harshly. So stay away, for your own good."

The bald man—Vince, apparently—spun on his heel and strode away. When he wasn't looming over Tesla, she could see what had changed his mind about having his friend come around the fence.

The cul-de-sac circle by the Landrigans' gate wasn't empty. A black SUV was parked there, with the engine running. DeMarco and Silas, the neighborhood kids Nick and Tesla had met the day before, were riding their bikes in slow circles nearby.

Witnesses. That's what had made the difference.

What would Vince and his friend Frank have done, Tesla had to wonder, if no one had been there to see it?

Tesla started toward the street, and Nick reluctantly followed her. They were going the same way Vince had just gone, and Nick's impulse was to run in the opposite direction.

As Nick and Tesla got closer to the road, the SUV parked there began cruising slowly away. The windows were tinted, so Nick couldn't see who was behind the wheel. The SUV was just a big box of black on wheels.

Silas and DeMarco followed it for a few seconds, then circled back toward Nick and Tesla.

"Was that the yell-y guy from the intercom?" Silas asked.

He nodded at Vince, who'd gone in through the front gate and was walking up the driveway toward the Landrigans' house. The Rottweilers trotted along on either side of him.

"Yeah," Nick said. "His name's Vince."

Silas and DeMarco looked impressed.

"We never got him mad enough to come out after us," DeMarco said. "He's almost as scary looking as his dogs."

"Jaws and Claws," Nick said.

Silas and DeMarco looked even more impressed.

"Whoa," said Silas.

"You still trying to get your stuff back?" said DeMarco.

Nick nodded. "It's not going very well."

"You ever hear of someone named Mr. Snugg?" Tesla asked.

The question was so out of the blue that DeMarco and Silas laughed.

"Mr. Snugg?" DeMarco said. He threw a dubious look at Tesla's electric pink backpack. "Sounds like the name of a cartoon cat."

"Ha, ha," Tesla said stiffly. "So you don't know him?"

Silas and DeMarco shook their heads.

"Who is he?" Silas asked.

"I don't know," Tesla said. "But I get the feeling he's not very nice."

"Oh?" said Silas.

"Yeah?" said DeMarco.

To them, "not very nice" was obviously *very* interesting.

"You guys notice a girl over there this week?" Tesla asked them. "About our age? Kind of skinny and pale?"

The boys shook their heads again, their eyes going wide. This was getting better and better.

"Did you see her?" DeMarco asked.

"Did you see *through* her?" asked Silas.

Tesla groaned and rolled her eyes.

"It's not a ghost, guys. She's real," Nick said. "Did *you* see her, Tez?"

Tesla nodded. "And you were right, Nick. Something's wrong. You can tell just by looking at her." She turned to DeMarco and Silas. "Have you ever noticed what time those renovator guys usually leave for the day?"

"Wait," Nick said. "You're not thinking of sneaking in there at night, are you?"

Tesla just threw her brother a cool noncommittal stare and said nothing.

"They never leave for the day," DeMarco said. "Not that we've ever seen."

"And Jaws and Claws are definitely there all the time," Silas added. "You can hear them barking at raccoons or skunks or whatever, way after dark."

"Is it normal for construction dudes to live in a house they're renovating?" Nick asked.

Everyone gave him a "How should I know?" look.

"As far as we can tell, they only leave the house once a day," Silas said.

"The van goes out every night around seven and comes back about half an hour later," said DeMarco.

Nick gave the boys a dubious smile. "Oh, come on.

119

Like you guys have been spending your summer vacation keeping track of local traffic."

DeMarco shrugged. "There's not much to do around here."

"Well, there is now," Tesla announced. "See ya later."

She turned and hurried off toward Uncle Newt's house.

All three boys just stood there for a moment watching her go. Nick recovered from his surprise first.

"Hey! Wait up!" he said.

"Yeah! Wait up!" said DeMarco.

"Yeah! Wait up!" said Silas.

Tesla didn't slow down, but that was okay. The boys managed to catch up, anyway.

Nick told Silas and DeMarco about the girl as they went. Despite his shyness, there was something about the boys that put him at ease. Maybe it was the enthusiasm with which they listened.

"Weird!" Silas said when Nick told them about the GO AWAY message the girl had flashed him.

NICK AND TESLA'S HIGH-VOLTAGE DANGER LAB

"Freaky!" DeMarco said when Nick told them about the way Vince had come chasing after him as his dogs ripped apart RoboSquirrel.

"Luminous!" Silas said when Tesla jumped in to mention Mr. Snugg.

"Luminous?" Nick and Tesla said.

"Doesn't that mean, like, 'spooky'?"

"I think you mean *ominous*," DeMarco said.

"That's it. Ominous!" said Silas. "There's creepier stuff going on over at the old Landrigan place than we ever thought!"

"Creepier than ghosts?" Nick asked.

"Oh. Well . . ."

Silas and DeMarco looked embarrassed.

"We never *really* believed that," DeMarco said.

"It made a good story," said Tesla. "But now we're after the truth."

By then they were in Uncle Newt's house, gathered outside the door to the laboratory.

"I think maybe you guys should wait here," Nick said to Silas and DeMarco. "Our uncle's sharing his lab with us, but I don't know if he'd want anyone else down there."

Silas and DeMarco stared at the signs on the door.

HAZARDOUS
FLAMMABLE
POISON
HIGH VOLTAGE
Etc.

"No problem," said DeMarco.

"In fact," said Silas, "can we wait outside?"

"Sure," said Nick. "But I don't know how long we'll be."

"Don't worry. We won't go anywhere," said Silas.

"We've been waiting for something to happen all summer," said DeMarco. "We're not going to miss it now!"

"It's nice having somebody on our side," said Nick as he and his sister went down the stairs to the lab.

"We'll see how nice it is if we ever really need their help."

"They wouldn't let us down. They seem like good guys."

"They're just bored. They'll lose interest in us the second something good comes on TV."

Nick shook his head. "Geez, Tez. And you always say I'm the negative one."

Tesla just started wandering around looking over the piles of equipment and random odds and ends.

"So," said Nick, "what are we down here for, anyway?"

"Proposition: Vince is a big jerk," she said.

"Accepted."

Tesla picked up a rusty old telescope, blew off some of the dust, sniffed it, then wrinkled her nose and put it back down.

"Proposition: Something odd is going on with that girl."

"Accepted," Nick said again.

"Proposition—"

"Whatever it is, I accept it!" Nick interrupted. "Just tell me why we're here!"

Tesla stopped her rummaging and turned to face her brother.

"Proposition," she said calmly.

"Agh!" groaned Nick, throwing up his hands in frustration.

Tesla plowed ahead anyway.

"If that girl needs help, we need to know it—and the best way to do that is to follow that van wherever it's been going."

Nick was still annoyed, but now he was intrigued, too.

"Not accepted," he said. "Why is following the van such a great idea?"

"Because it's something we can do without getting chased by Jaws and Claws."

"Ahhh." Nick nodded. "Accepted."

He started looking around the lab, too.

"So we're here," he said, "to figure out how to follow the van."

"Exactly. We need a van tracker. Something simple, nonelectronic. Like maybe . . ."

Tesla waved a hand at a pyramid of grungy paint cans.

"Hole in can, secure can to truck, follow dribbles?" Nick said. "Maybe . . . only we've gotta figure whoever's driving the van is going to walk around to the back sooner or later. Wouldn't he notice the fresh paint he's stepping in?"

Tesla slumped and moved on. "Probably."

"What we need is invisible van tracking," Nick said.

"Yeah. But if it's invisible, how do we see it?"

Nick cleared his throat.

When Tesla turned toward him, she saw that he was holding up a bucket filled with discarded orange highlighter markers. The bottoms seemed to have been sawed off, probably so that Uncle Newt could remove the ink and use it to color his spray-on clothes.

"Remember those cool jack-o'-lanterns Mom made one year?" he said. "The ones that seemed to glow under the right kind of light?"

Nick pointed at a small wandlike device nestled in with a bunch of other techno doodads on a work-table nearby.

Tesla grinned.

"Proposition: You are a genius."

"Accepted," said Nick.

SEMI-INVISIBLE
NIGHTTIME
VAN TRACKER

THE STUFF:

- 1 fresh highlighter marker
- Scissors
- 1 zip-top sandwich bag
- 1 pushpin
- Duct tape
- 1 battery-powered black light (available at many hardware or party stores)
- Pliers

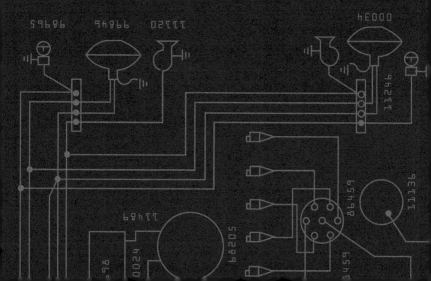

THE SETUP

1. Using the pliers, squeeze the base of the highlighter marker. The stopper at the end (usually white) should pop out.

2. Carefully remove the marker's inner dye pack.

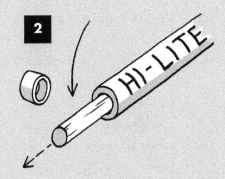

3. Standing over a sink, cut the dye pack into three or four pieces and place them inside the sandwich bag.

4. Add 1½ cups (237 ml) of water to the bag and zip it shut.

5. Give the dye time to mix with the water.

THE FINAL STEPS

1. Use the duct tape to attach the bag of dye to the underside of the back bumper on the vehicle you want to track.

2. Use the pushpin to poke a single hole into one bottom corner of the bag. As the liquid drips out of the bag, it will leave a trail of fluorescent dye that will glow under the black light. (A black light emits ultraviolet light, which is invisible to humans. But our eyes can see how the light reacts to certain vibrant neon colors, like the kinds in most highlighter markers.) The bag should last about 10 minutes, so don't put the hole in it too soon.

3. Follow the trail.

SIRINGO BROS
HOME RENOVATORS

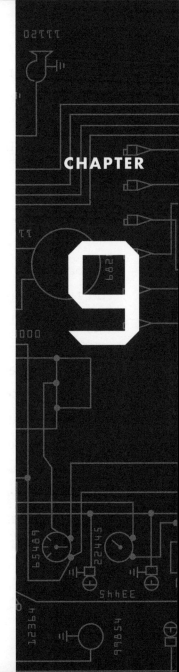

Nick had never been on a stakeout before. It might have been kind of cool if he hadn't been riding a purple paisley bicycle built for a girl half his size.

There had been only one bike in Uncle Newt's garage: an old-fashioned ten-speed buried under so many cobwebs it looked like a giant spider had tried to wrap it in a cocoon. Nick and Tesla flipped a coin for it, and Tesla won. Which was why Nick got stuck with the bike that belonged to DeMarco's little sister. They'd been able to get the training wheels off, but the flowery basket on the handlebars wouldn't budge.

"Pedaling this little thing is killing my knees," Nick said as he started another wobbly circuit around the cul-de-sac. He was hoping Tesla would offer to take turns on the ten-speed.

Instead, she just cruised past him and said, "It was either Elesha's bike or the Big Wheel."

"I know, I know," Nick grumbled.

He threw another surreptitious (he hoped) glance at the Landrigans' driveway. They had to make sure they were in just the right spot when the van left that evening. Which is why they'd been riding around and around by the Landrigans' front gate for the past twenty minutes.

"So, how long are you guys gonna be visiting your uncle?" Silas asked. "A week or two?"

"The whole summer," Nick said.

"The whole summer? Here?" said DeMarco. He looked like he pitied them. "Why?"

"Our parents are government scientists," Nick said. "They got sent to Uzbekistan."

"What's in Oozebeckyland?" Silas asked.

"Soybeans," said Tesla. "Really well irrigated soybeans."

"Sounds thrilling," said DeMarco, his voice dripping with sarcasm. "Why couldn't they take you with them?"

Neither Nick nor Tesla answered. They just looked at each other, obviously thinking the same thing.

Yeah . . . why not?

"Whoa," said Silas. "Here we go."

The white Siringo Bros. van was coming around the house.

The kids sped up their circling, yelling bogus trash talk at one another as they fake-raced around the cul-de-sac.

"Eat my dust!"

"Save your breath for pedaling—you'll need it!"

"Real cool bike, Nick! What's the matter? Your tricycle have a flat?"

"Hey!"

The gate started to swing open automatically as the van drew near.

They'd have to time this operation just right.

DeMarco broke away from the pack and doubled back toward the Landrigan place.

"Shortcut!" he called over his shoulder.

"Cheater!" the others yelled at him.

They all pretended not to notice that the van was driving past the gate and would be easing out into the street any second.

The big, scruffy guy—Frank—was behind the wheel. He honked his horn as DeMarco headed straight for him.

It was up to DeMarco now.

"Don't worry. He can handle it," Silas had said when they'd hatched the plan. "He's doing X Games–type stuff on his bike all the time, and he's only broken three bones."

That hadn't reassured Nick much, but Tesla had nodded and said, "All right, DeMarco. Try not to break number four."

And now there DeMarco was, looking at the van in fake surprise, swerving to the left in fake panic, and then doing a very real wipeout with what sounded like a real scream.

DeMarco's X Games–type practice paid off. He ended up sprawling in the street right where he was supposed to: not close enough to the van to risk getting hit by it, but squarely in front of it so it couldn't go around him.

Frank hit the brakes, and the van screeched to a halt.

"Waaaaaaaaa!" DeMarco wailed. He wrapped his hands around his right knee and began rocking and sobbing. "It hurrrrrrrts!"

Tesla and Nick and Silas pedaled toward him furiously.

"DeMarco!"

"Are you all right?"

"Is any bone sticking out?"

They hopped off their bikes and gathered around

their fallen friend.

Frank leaned out the driver's side window.

"Would you get out of the way?" he said.

"That's real nice!" Tesla snapped at him. "You practically flatten an innocent kid in the street, and then all you have to say is, 'Get out of the way.'"

"Oh, all he's got is a skinned knee. And you kids shouldn't be hanging around out here anyway."

"This is a public street, mister!" Silas said. "You don't own the road!"

"Yeah!" Nick added. It just seemed like the kind of thing *someone* would say, under the circumstances.

"I wa-wa-wannnnnnt my m-mommy!" DeMarco blubbered.

Nick thought he was laying it on a bit thick, but now wasn't the time for acting critiques.

DeMarco's seven-year-old sister Elesha stepped out around the van. She walked up to her brother and looked down at him gravely, shaking her head.

"Mom's gonna kill you if you messed up your bike."

DeMarco started crying harder.

"Oh, for cryin' out loud," Frank groaned. He gave the horn two quick honks. "Move it! I've got somewhere I need to be!"

"Okay, okay!" Tesla said. "What's the rush? You got some old ladies to run over?"

She helped DeMarco up, and he started hobbling toward the curb as the other kids moved their bikes. The second they were out of Frank's way, he stomped on the gas and roared off up the street.

Tesla turned to Elesha.

"Did you get the drip bag attached to the back bumper the way we showed you?" she asked.

"Of course. It was easy."

Elesha stuck out a hand, palm up.

Tesla paid her three dollars for hiding in the trees with the tracking dye, plus another two for letting Nick "rent" her bike.

"Pleasure doing business with you," Elesha said as she folded the bills and stuffed them in her pocket. She cocked an eyebrow at her brother. "Good acting, crybaby. Or was it acting?"

DeMarco showed her his fist.

"I'll show you what real crying is, if you want," he said.

"Ha. As if you'd *dare*."

Elesha turned her back to DeMarco, flipped her

cornrows over her shoulders and went sashaying away.

"Your sister is one tough second-grader," Nick said.

DeMarco shivered. "You should meet the one in kindergarten."

Silas walked out into the road, crouched down, and wiped a hand over the asphalt.

"I think there's a little ink here," he said. "But I can barely see it."

Tesla stared off at the horizon. The sky was starting to go from pale blue to pink-streaked orange. Before long, night would fall.

"Just wait," Tesla said. "You'll see it."

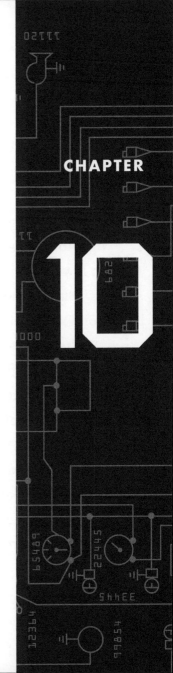

10

"I still don't see it," Silas said.

It was dusk, and the world had gone gray.

"The ink doesn't glow in the dark, remember?" Tesla said. "We need this."

She pulled Uncle Newt's black light out of her kitty backpack. It looked like a big blue test tube with black backing and a strap. When Tesla turned it on, the tube shined with a soft eerie light.

Tesla knelt down and slowly moved the black light over the road. Nick, Silas, and DeMarco all leaned in over her shoulder.

"I don't know," Silas said. "I *still* don't . . . whoa!"

Fluorescent orange splatters appeared in the black light's glow.

"Nice one, Nick," Tesla said. She stood up and handed her brother the black light. "Now attach that to Elesha's bike, and we'll get going."

She pulled a roll of duct tape from her backpack and gave that to Nick, too. He started taping the black light to the front fender of Elesha's bike, adjusting it so it would shine down and to the left.

"Elesha's not gonna be happy if she catches you doing that," Silas said, glancing around nervously. "You're supposed to be riding it, not customizing it."

"Remind me—why does the light have to be on my sister's bike, anyway?" asked DeMarco.

"Because of all our bikes, it's the closest to the ground," Tesla told him.

"And remind *me*," said Nick as he finished pressing down the last silvery strip of tape. "Why am I the one who has to ride this teeny little thing?"

"Because you lost the coin toss. And it was your idea."

"Oh. Right," Nick said. "I'm a genius."

He suddenly didn't sound very happy about it.

He got on Elesha's bike and began pedaling awkwardly away. As he went, little beads of bright orange glowed below him on the pavement.

Half Moon Bay was a small coastal town surrounded on three sides by thick groves of tall trees, so the road the kids ended up on wasn't *that* busy. Their little caravan got honked at only once every, oh, sixty seconds or so. And the cars that whooshed by less than two feet from Nick's hand weren't going any faster than, say, thirty or so miles an hour. Fast enough to squish him, sure, but not so fast that the wind they whipped up knocked him over.

It was quite a joyride. Nick spent most of the time telling himself he shouldn't always be so quick to share his bright ideas.

"What if he went on the interstate?" Nick heard DeMarco say behind him.

"You and Silas said the van's always gone about half an hour," Tesla replied. "How far could he be going?"

"A lot farther than I can go," Silas wheezed. The

last quarter mile had been uphill.

"Look," Tesla said, "even if the trail does lead to a highway, at least we'll know which way the guy was going."

"Would that really help us?" Nick said.

Either his sister didn't hear him or she didn't have an answer.

"Hey!" Nick blurted out.

The glowing trail had veered right, away from the road, and Nick had to swerve to stay with it.

He coasted down a gently sloping drive into a small parking lot. Tesla, Silas, and DeMarco fanned out around him as they followed.

The lot was deserted, and there was only a single building: a long single-level store built to look like a log cabin. A sign on the roof said GOLDEN STATE ANITQUES & COLLECTIBLES. A sign in the window said CLOSED.

The fluorescent trail didn't stop out front. Instead, it wound around to the back of the building, out of sight of the road. Nick started to follow it but then veered off when he saw headlights flash up ahead.

"Someone's coming this way!" he cried out. "We gotta hide!"

The other kids followed as Nick cut over toward the antiques store. Just as they reached the front door, the Siringo Bros. van came around the side of the building. Nick half expected it to stop so that blustery muscle-bound Frank could pop out and demand to know why they'd been following him. But the van kept going. It went out to the exit, turned left onto the road, and headed in the direction they'd just come—back to the Landrigan place, presumably.

So their tracking system had worked! They'd figured out where Frank was going.

An empty parking lot behind a closed antiques store.

Nick wasn't sure if he should find that really, really mysterious or really, really disappointing.

"Come on," Tesla said, getting her bike rolling again. "Let's see what's back there."

What was back there was nothing. Just the rear of the store and a few more parking spots out of sight of the road and, picking up where the pavement stopped, lush forest thick with ferns, moss, and the tallest trees Nick had ever seen.

Nick rode around in circles until he found the fluorescent orange trail again. It ended in a big glowing puddle. The kids stopped in a circle around it.

"Is there anything special about this antiques store?" Tesla asked Silas and DeMarco.

They both shrugged and mumbled "I dunno."

"There are lots of places like it around here," said Silas. "But they're for tourists, not kids."

"We're not big antiques collectors," said DeMarco.

Silas nodded vigorously. "Yeah, really. Don't you think old stuff is creepy? Like, you know those old porcelain dolls? The ones that are all white with the big staring eyes? They look like vampires or zombies or something. I heard one time that the hair on them is real. As in real hair from real people. Isn't that the ickiest thing you ever—"

"All right, Silas, thanks for sharing," Tesla said. She waved a hand at the pool of luminescent water at their feet. "But maybe we should be focusing on this?"

"Oh. Right." Silas looked down at the puddle. "Sure is orange."

"And big," said Nick. "Frank must have been parked here for a while for that much ink to drip out."

"But the store's closed," said DeMarco. "Why would he come here just to sit in his van?"

"Maybe he didn't," Tesla said. She leaned over the

handlebars of her bike, staring at something on the ground. "Shine the light over there."

Nick walked Elesha's bike toward the spot Tesla was looking at. An orange shape began shining on the ground, then another, then another.

Footprints. Big ones.

They led from the puddle out toward the trees. The trail ended with a final footprint that shimmered brighter, and with sharper edges, than the rest. Bits of shattered plastic were mixed in with it, glowing orange. More footprints led from there back to where the van had been parked.

Tesla squatted and picked up one of the bigger shards of plastic. She held it under the black light.

"There's something printed on this. Like a manufacturer's name," she said. "It looks like . . . Sushami."

Silas scowled and scratched his head. "Isn't that, like, raw fish?"

"I don't think Frank drove out here just to stomp on a box of sushi," said Nick.

"No," said his sister. "But he did stomp on something. Maybe something he got out of the back of the van."

Nick nodded. "Makes sense. He had to have gone

around to the back, where the bag and the puddle were, or we wouldn't be seeing these footprints."

DeMarco shook his head. "No. Does *not* make sense. Why would he come all the way out here just to bust up a *sushami*, whatever that is? He could do that back at the Landrigan place. And why do it at the same time every day?"

Tesla opened her mouth to answer, then froze. It looked like she'd expected something brilliant to pop out, but it never showed up.

"I have no idea," she finally said.

Nick stifled a sigh.

They'd come all this way looking for answers, and what had they found? Some footprints and busted-up plastic.

And more questions.

The ride back to their uncle's neighborhood was both easier and harder than before. Nick didn't have to worry about keeping the black light pointed at the pavement anymore, so he could put a little more distance between himself and the road. And they were headed mostly downhill.

But it was pitch black now, and though Elesha's bike had reflectors, Nick would have been more comfortable with a flashing neon sign strapped to his back.

KIDS BIKING!!!
DON'T HIT!!!

"Have you noticed that big black car?" DeMarco asked.

"All the cars look big and black to me," said Nick.

"What big black car?" said Tesla.

"Behind us. It's been there for, like, a mile."

Nick looked back and saw Tesla and Silas looking back, too.

About thirty yards behind them was a large, dark, boxy shape. It was cruising so slowly along the two-lane road that other cars were whipping around to pass it.

"Looks like an SUV," said Silas.

"There was a black SUV—" Nick began.

"—parked near the Landrigans' house this morning," Tesla finished for him.

A name popped into Nick's head, and he said it out loud.

"Mr. Snugg. The mastermind."

"Don't jump to conclusions, Mr. Sunshine," Tesla said. "(A) We don't know it's Mr. Snugg. (B) We don't know that Mr. Snugg is the mastermind behind anything. And (C) 'mastermind' is a really silly word."

"Well, (D) I've still got a *bad* feeling about this," said Nick.

"(E) Me, too," said DeMarco.

"(G) I'm freaking out here," said Silas.

Nick was about to point out that he'd skipped F, but he stopped himself. There were bigger things to worry about just then.

He looked back again. The other kids were all looking back, too.

The black SUV was still behind them.

Another car pulled out around it and cruised off down the road. Yet still the SUV didn't speed up.

"It's like he's waiting till there's no one else around," Nick said. "When it'll just be him and us out here in the dark."

"Okay," said Tesla. "Now you're freaking *me* out."

"Let's get out of here!" Silas said.

He shot past on Nick's right, pedaling furiously. A second later, DeMarco and Tesla zipped by, too.

"Come on!" Tesla called over her shoulder.

"I'm going as fast as I can!" Nick shouted back.

It was true. The harder he pumped his legs, the more his feet just slipped off the little pedals of Elesha's bike.

The road went quiet and dark as Silas, DeMarco, and Tesla drew farther away. There were no cars passing them, and none coming in the opposite direction, either. The road was deserted.

Almost.

Everything around Nick suddenly lit up. Headlights were drawing up close behind him.

He looked back again.

The SUV was still there—and it was speeding up.

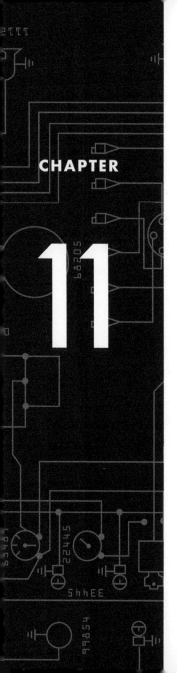

"Shortcut!" DeMarco yelled, and he cut his bike right and disappeared into the blackness beside the road.

Silas and Tesla followed him.

The light around Nick grew brighter. The headlights were getting closer.

He had a choice: The danger he knew or the danger he didn't.

He chose the latter and veered off into the void.

He found himself careening down a steep slope. It must have been rocky, because every few seconds he ran over something big and hard that sent the bike's banana

seat slamming up into him like a fist hitting *way* below the belt.

"Woo hooooo!" he heard DeMarco hoot.

"Ow ow OW ow ow OW OW ow ow ow OW," said Nick.

Eventually, the ground leveled out and Nick was whizzing over nice soft grass and weeds. Up ahead he could see three silhouettes as they whooshed through the brush, headed toward what looked like another road. There were no cars in sight.

Then lights appeared.

The SUV was turning onto the street ahead.

"Go, go, go, go, go!" DeMarco yelled.

He zipped over the road and whooshed into the brush on the other side. A moment later, Silas and Tesla did the same.

Nick was thirty feet behind them, and the SUV was getting closer.

Nick tried to focus on pedaling firmly, not frantically. Breathing deeply, not panting. Muttering "Come on, come on, come *on*," not screaming his head off as he popped out onto the road.

And it worked. He reached the other side before the SUV could shoot ahead and flatten him.

The ground Nick found himself riding over was even rougher than before, and it looked like DeMarco was leading the kids straight into some trees. Yet Nick just kept pedaling as hard as he could. Better to smack face-first into a giant redwood than stop and see what the driver of that SUV was up to now.

"Single file!" Silas called out as he reached the trees, and DeMarco, Tesla, and Nick fell into line behind him.

A second later, they were all bumping along a rough trail cutting through the forest. It was narrower than Nick would have liked—he could feel branches and cobwebs and who-knew-what brushing over him in the gloom—but there was no way a sport utility vehicle could fit on it, and that counted for a lot.

The trail emptied out onto a grassy hill. DeMarco and Silas whooped triumphantly as they rode out onto it.

They'd made it! They were safe at last!

"Wooo—" Nick said.

He never got to "hooo!" Instead, he let loose with an "Ahhh!" as his front tire rammed into something in the dark and the bike stopped cold. Nick's momentum sent him flying over the handlebars and crashing face-first into what felt like moist, sticky sand.

"Nick!" he heard Tesla shout.

Almost instantly, she was by his side. DeMarco, too.

"Are you all right?" Tesla said.

"I think so," Nick said as he pushed himself up and brushed himself off.

He could see now what he'd hit: a sandbox he'd noticed earlier that day.

They were in DeMarco's backyard.

DeMarco was looking down at the little bike Nick had just been catapulted from. The front wheel had been bent into an oval by the impact.

"Oh, man," DeMarco said, shaking his head. "Elesha's gonna kill you."

Nick looked back at the trail. Through the trees, he could see the distant twinkle of headlights moving away, then fading into the night.

"Well, she'll have to move fast," Nick said. "It looks like she's got competition."

The kids had less than a minute to discuss what to do next. "Should we tell any grown-ups?" was barely out of Silas's mouth when the patio light came on and a sharp voice called out, "DeMarco Martin Davison, where have you been? Why can you never remember to tell me where you're going? Are you *trying* to get yourself in trouble? Is that Silas with you? Did *he* remember to tell his parents where he'd be? Have either of you ever stopped to ask yourselves why you're getting grounded all the time? Is it some big mystery to you? Do you even know what time it is? Do you have any idea how worried I've been? Do you? Well? Do *you*?"

And on and on DeMarco's mother went. She didn't really seem to expect any answers. She just kept pelting her son with questions as he trudged toward the house and went inside.

The patio light went off.

"I'd better get home, too," said Silas. "Mrs. Davison's probably calling my mom right now. If I'm not back within five minutes, you won't see me outside till August."

He started to get on his bike, then stopped and squinted at Nick's face.

"You might want to take a shower," he said. "Every cat in the neighborhood visits that sandbox."

Nick brought up a hand and felt a clump of soggy sand still stuck to his right cheek.

"Ew!" he said.

"See ya!" Silas said as he rode away. "Don't get into any more car chases until DeMarco and I find you tomorrow!"

"We won't!" Tesla said. She gave him a good-night wave and then turned to her brother. "You know, you were right about those guys. They're all right."

Nick barely heard her. He'd just noticed all the damp sand in his hair.

"*Ew!*"

Nick and Tesla skulked and slinked and sneaked their way toward Uncle Newt's house, just to be safe. But they never spotted the black SUV . . . even though Nick realized when they were halfway home that the driver might know exactly where they were going.

"He saw us in front of the Landrigan place, so he knows we live nearby," he said, still rubbing obsessively at his hair. "In fact, now that I think of it, he might know *exactly* where we live."

"How would he know that?"

"The name we gave our air rocket."

"Why would that . . . ? Oh."

Tesla had painted *The Albert and Martha Holt* right on the side of the bottle.

Uncle Newt's last name was Holt, too.

"Yeah. *Oh*," Nick said. "If Mr. Snugg got hold of that rocket, two minutes on the Internet would be all he'd need to find us."

"Like I said before, we don't know it was Snugg in the SUV," Tesla said. "But if it was and he'd been able to look up Uncle Newt's address, why would he try to get us on the road just now? He could just wait at the house for us."

Nick pondered that a moment.

"Maybe that's the back-up plan," he said.

He and Tesla stopped and looked at each other.

After that, they started skulking and slinking and sneaking even slower, with lots of glances over their shoulders.

When Nick and Tesla finally slipped safely inside their uncle's house, they found it even more cluttered than before. The dining room was packed with boxes and bags and stacks of cans and cartons. There were soups, cereals, peanut butter, and ramen noodles by the case and a stack of video games and DVDs that reached almost to the ceiling.

"I didn't know what you guys like," Uncle Newt said. "So I just got one of everything."

"Oh, my gosh, Uncle Newt," said Tesla, looking around in wonderment. "This must have cost you a fortune."

Uncle Newt shrugged dismissively. "Oh, I don't care. You know those new bacon straws everyone's gone nuts for? That was me. Prechewed food, too."

"Bacon straws?" said Nick.

"Prechewed food?" said Tesla.

Their uncle looked puzzled.

"Those aren't popular?"

Nick and Tesla shook their heads.

"Well, I sold the patents, anyway," Uncle Newt said. "And dozens of others. I guess not all of it has made it to the public yet, but I'm doing okay. Say, wanna try some prechewed food? It's all the flavor with none of the work!"

"No, thanks," Nick and Tesla said at the same time.

"Try it. You'll like it. Comes in a tube, just like astronaut food. You can even eat it with a bacon straw!"

Eureka the bald cat sauntered into the room and began sniffing Nick in a way that seemed to make him very, very nervous.

"I've got to take a shower," said Nick, hurrying toward the staircase. "But after that, I'd love some Cocoa Puffs!"

Uncle Newt looked disappointed.

"Sure. If that's what you really want," he said. "We've got fresh milk, too."

"Great! I'll be back in a minute. I'm starving!"

Nick went bounding up the stairs.

Tesla was hungry, too. But she had something on her mind other than cereal.

"Uncle Newt," she said, "what would you say if I told you something weird was going on around here?"

"I'd say, 'Tell me something I don't know.' When Julie from next door saw me unloading all this stuff, she came over to ask where her new garden gnome was. And when I told her I didn't have one, she got mad! The woman's certifiable."

"I'm not thinking of Julie. It's . . . it's . . . oh, never mind."

"Come on, Tesla. Lay it on me. I'm a good listener."

Tesla didn't mean to look skeptical, but she must have, all the same.

"Really!" Uncle Newt said. "I know I can seem a little checked-out sometimes, but I want to be here for you." He stood a little straighter and squared his shoulders, like a soldier reporting for duty. "Please. Tell me whatever you'd tell your mom and dad if they were here."

Of course, the first thing Tesla would say to her mom and dad would be, *Why did you send us here and can't we go home now, please, please, please?*

Tesla took in a deep breath and told Uncle Newt what she would have said to her parents after all that.

And he *was* a good listener. He didn't even get distracted when Nick came downstairs wrapped in a towel and began listening in over a bowl overflowing with Cocoa Puffs *and* Golden Grahams *and* Frosted Flakes.

When Tesla was done telling Uncle Newt about the rocket and the pendant and the girl and Vince and Frank and their dogs and Mr. Snugg and the black SUV, he sat quietly at the dining room table for a moment, hands steepled, brow furrowed.

"It is weird," he finally said. "But . . . 'We are to admit no more causes of natural things than such as are both true and sufficient to explain their appearances.'"

"Sou li Uh-huh raoh," Nick said through a mouthful of soggy cereal.

"Excuse me?"

Nick swallowed and tried again.

"Sounds like Occam's razor."

"Exactly," Uncle Newt said with an approving nod. "I was quoting Isaac Newton's version of it."

"Mom and Dad used to talk about Occam's razor all the time," Tesla said. "'Simple explanations are usually better than complicated ones.' It's a good rule, I guess . . . but what does it have to do with us?"

Uncle Newt shrugged. "Maybe Vince or Frank is Mr. Snugg. Maybe they're just trying to protect all the expensive new fixtures they're putting in the house. Maybe the girl's just an unfriendly Landrigan or Vince or Frank's unfriendly daughter."

"And the black SUV?" Tesla said.

Uncle Newt stood up and headed for the kitchen. "That's what I'm going to call the police about."

"Thanks, Uncle Newt," Tesla said.

At least he was taking *something* she'd said seriously.

While Uncle Newt talked on the phone in the kitchen, Tesla looked over the booty in the dining room. Watching her brother shovel down gloopy brown sludge turned her off cereal, so she looked through the soups instead.

It was a good thing she liked chicken noodle. Her uncle had bought two hundred cans. It was as if he wasn't stocking up for a summer visit: He was preparing for a siege.

Tesla was about to go hunting for a can opener when Uncle Newt returned.

"Your new friends seem to have told the same story to their parents," he said. "Apparently, I was the third person to call about a black SUV following kids. So, don't you worry. The police are going to be on the lookout for it."

"Excellent," said Nick.

"Good," said Tesla.

Yet, they must not have sounded sincere enough.

"Believe me, guys," Uncle Newt said. "There is no skullduggery in Half Moon Bay. We're boring. Nothing sinister or dangerous ever happens around—"

There was a muffled *boom*, and the house shook.

"Uh-oh," said Uncle Newt. "That would be the kiln blowing up again. It's fine up to three hundred degrees Celsius, but after that? Kerblooey!"

A wisp of smoke swirled into the room.

"Excuse me."

Uncle Newt hurried off to the lab.

Tesla turned to her brother. "Feeling reassured?"

"Not really."

"Me, neither."

"So, what do we do?"

Tesla sucked in a deep breath. By the time she was blowing it out again, she had a plan.

"First, I am going to eat two cans of chicken noodle soup," she said. "Then we're going to make sure whoever was in that SUV doesn't come get us before we can go get him."

CHRISTMAS-IS-OVER INTRUDER ALERT SYSTEM

THE STUFF:

- 1 string of old Christmas tree lights (or a 12-volt LED bulb from any electronics store)

- 1 9-volt battery

- 2 quarters

- Paper

- Tape

- String

- Scissors

- 1 thin, flexible, plastic-coated wire available at any electronics store (the length will vary depending on your needs)

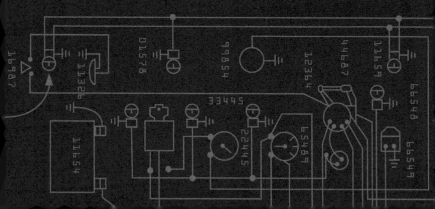

THE SETUP

1. One end of the alarm system will be near a door. The other end will be in your Intruder Alarm Notification Center (a.k.a., wherever you want the alarm light to be). Determine how much wire you'll need by measuring from the bottom of the door to the spot you've chosen for the light. You might want to give yourself a little extra wire, so you can tuck it away out of sight.

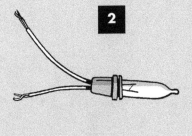

2. Be sure the old Christmas tree lights are unplugged. Use scissors to snip off a single light. Leave a little extra wire (about 1 inch [2.5 cm]) hanging from light.

3. Test the light by touching each end of the wire running from it to the 9-volt battery. The bulb should come on.

4. Cut two equal lengths of wire based on your measurements from step 1. We will call them Wire A and Wire B.

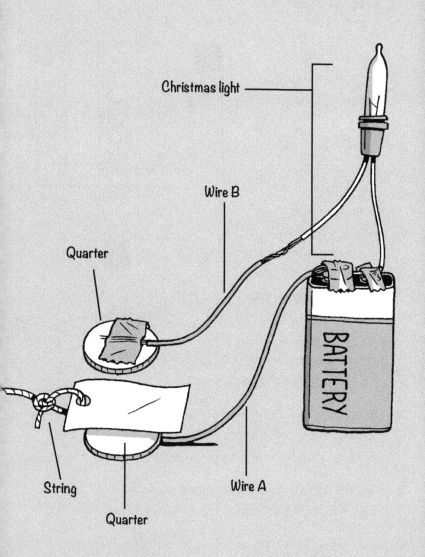

Christmas light

Wire B

Quarter

Quarter

String

Wire A

BATTERY

5. Use the scissors to remove ½ inch (1.25 cm) of plastic casing from the ends of Wire A, Wire B, and the Christmas light wires. Ask an adult if you have trouble with this step.

6. Tape one end of Wire A to either metal tab on the battery.

7. Twist one end of Wire B onto one of the light bulb wires.

8. Tape the other light bulb wire onto the remaining metal tab on top of the battery.

9. Tape the remaining ends of Wires A and B to separate quarters. When the quarters touch, the bulb should light up.

THE FINAL STEPS

1. Place the battery/bulb assembly in your Intruder Alarm Notification Center.

2. Put the quarters near the door.

3. Attach a string to a small piece of paper.

4. Place the paper between the quarters to keep them from touching.

5. Tape the other end of the string to the door so that, if the door's opened, the paper will be pulled away, allowing the quarters to touch and thus turning on the light.

6. Wait for an intruder.

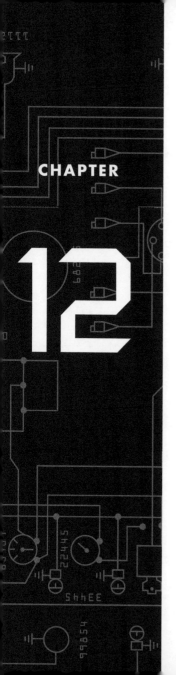

12

Nick and Tesla got the light for their alarm system from the Christmas tree in the hallway.

"Uncle Newt's gonna be mad when he finds out we cut this up," Nick said as they unwound the string of lights from the tree.

"He's not going to notice," said Tesla. "It's June. We have plenty of time to buy him new lights before he gets in the Christmas spirit again."

"I'm not so sure, Tez. . . ."

Uncle Newt was singing "Rockin' around the Christmas Tree" (or, as he called it, "Boppin' along the

Christmas Thing") as he cleared the smoke from the kiln explosion out of the basement.

Nick and Tesla realized they only needed to wire the back door. The front, Nick remembered, already had an alarm of sorts: the pressure-sensitive doorbell ringer under the welcome mat. If Mr. Snugg or Vince or Frank tried to get in that way, Nick and Tesla would know they were there before they even touched the lock, let alone picked it.

After testing their intruder alert light to their satisfaction (Nick's satisfaction requiring about five more trial runs than Tesla's), they went around the house and made sure all the windows were closed and locked. Once that was done, Nick could relax. Or try to relax, anyway.

"I think I'm going to read for a while," said Nick. "In the bathroom. With the airlock sealed."

"I'm going to find Mr. Snugg," said Tesla.

"*What?* We spend an hour making sure we're safe from the bad guys, then you want to go out in the middle of the night and look for—"

Nick stopped himself before he could say "the mastermind." It was embarrassing enough that he'd just said "the bad guys."

"—the dude with the funky name," he said instead.

"Who said anything about going out?"

Tesla pointed at a scuffed-up laptop on the kitchen counter.

"Oh. *That* kind of looking," Nick said. "All right. Let's go."

The last Google search anyone had done on the laptop, Nick and Tesla discovered, had been "food kids cheap easy healthy."

"At least he included 'healthy,'" Nick said.

"Maybe that's how we ended up with fifty gallons of chicken noodle soup," said Tesla.

She typed in a search of her own.

"Snugg Half Moon Bay California."

The first hundred or so results were for local hotels and bed-and-breakfasts, all of which claimed to be "snug."

"Try an online phone directory," Nick suggested.

Tesla quickly found one and searched for anybody named Snugg in Half Moon Bay.

Nothing.

She widened the search to anybody named Snugg in Northern California.

Nothing.

She widened the search to anybody named Snugg in the whole state.

Finally, they got a hit.

"Hey, look at that," Nick said. "There's a Mildred A. Snugg in Los Angeles. That's only . . . what? Four hundred miles from here? Are you sure the girl didn't write 'Ms. Snugg'?"

Tesla glowered at her brother. "Are you being sarcastic?"

Nick thought it safer to say "No." So that's what he did.

Tesla tried searching for Siringo Bros. Home Renovators next. A website for the company came up.

"They're based in Sacramento," she said as she and Nick skimmed through the site. "I don't think that's very close to here, either."

"And I don't see any mention of a Vince or Frank Siringo."

"Well, we don't know that Vince and Frank are the Siringo brothers. They might just work for them."

"Sure," Nick said. "They're such nice, charming

guys, of course the Siringos would hire them."

"They can be mean to *us*, Nick. Kids don't get home renovations. Maybe they're sweet as pie to other grown-ups."

"Yeah," Nick said. "Maybe."

Tesla went back to Google.

"One more search. . . ."

She typed in "Sushami."

That had its own website, too, it turned out. The Sushami Corporation was "one of the world's leading manufacturers of budget-range mobile communications devices."

"They make cheap cell phones?" Nick said.

"Looks like it."

"So Frank leaves the Landrigan place at the same time every night so he can drive to a parking lot and jump up and down on a phone?"

Nick was just being sarcastic again. But to his surprise, Tesla nodded.

"He did it where no one could see, remember?" she said. "At the edge of the lot so he could throw the biggest pieces into the woods."

"And he'd do that because . . . ?"

"I have no idea." Tesla rubbed her chin. "I wonder

what Occam's razor would say."

"You want the simplest possible explanation?" Nick said. "How about we're nuts and none of this is actually happening?"

Tesla kept rubbing her chin. "I'll consider it."

She closed the laptop and started toward the stairs.

Tesla read in bed. Nick tried to, but he just ended up staring blankly at his book. He was thinking about big black SUVs and big black Rottweilers and big black holes in the ground he didn't want anyone filling with meddling kids.

And he was thinking about the girl. There seemed to be a big black void around her, too. Mystery, you could call it. Menace.

Danger.

Eventually, it was time to turn out the light and go to sleep—though Nick expected to spend the night thinking the same big black thoughts while old slices of pizza slowly decomposed beneath him.

Whoever had been driving that SUV was still out

there somewhere. Their first enemy. Not the "She said my hair looked stupid" or "He cut in front of me in the lunch line" kind. A *real* enemy. The kind who wants to hurt you . . . or worse.

Nick wondered if he should be mad at his mom and dad for shipping him off into this mess. After a while, he decided it wasn't their fault.

But he'd hate soybeans till the day he died.

Nick dreamed he was at the North Pole.

"Rudolph," he moaned in his sleep. "Stop looking at me like that. I didn't say you couldn't play any reindeer games. Really. Come on. Back off. I said, back—"

Nick's eyes flew open, and he wasn't looking at a murderously furious glowing-nosed reindeer anymore. He was looking at a single red light shining out in utter darkness. It took him a moment to grasp what it was: the Christmas light they'd taped to the back of the door before going to bed.

Suddenly, he was very, *very* awake.

"Tez," he whispered. "Intruder alert."

He heard his sister stir . . . then begin snoring softly again.

She always was a deeper sleeper.

"Someone is in the house," Nick hissed. "*Tesla.*"

Nick heard his sister sit up straight and throw off her covers.

"Let's do this thing!" she said.

"Huh? Do what thing?"

"I . . . I don't know."

A moment of silence passed while Tesla apparently finished waking up.

"Oh, geez, the intruder light's on," she finally said. "Someone's in the house."

"That's what I've been trying to tell you. What do we do now?"

They'd improvised their own alarm system, but they'd neglected to discuss what to do if it actually went off.

"Now . . . well . . . I guess we *do* do this thing," Tesla said.

"*What thing?*"

Nick was hoping it might be: barricade the door and start screaming. But he heard his sister stand and start moving slowly, quietly toward the hallway.

"Tesla," Nick whispered. "When the bad guys come to get you, you don't go meet them halfway. You run and hide."

"No one's going to get us. We're going to scare them off. But I want to see their faces first."

A black shape moved in front of the alarm light.

"Tesla."

She opened the door, tiptoed into the hall, and headed for the stairs.

"Tez," Nick said softly. "*Tez*."

She didn't turn back.

"Dang," Nick said.

He got up and followed her.

By the time he caught up, she was halfway down the stairs. Below them, moonlight shining through the windows sliced into the darkness of the first floor in long straight lines. Nick couldn't see anyone, but that didn't mean they weren't there. There were still plenty of pitch-black shadows to hide in.

Tesla stopped.

Nick was more than happy to stop, too. He and his sister stood there for a while listening, watching. Sweating, in Nick's case.

"I don't see anything," Nick whispered.

Tesla shushed him, then slowly raised a hand and pointed toward the back of the house.

Nick looked that way and saw nothing. He finally heard something, though.

Floorboards creaking. Footsteps. A door opening? Or was it closing? Or maybe opening and closing at the same time? How could that be unless . . .?

Two doors were being opened and/or closed? By two intruders?

Nick heard a man muttering, the words indistinct but his tone gruff, angry. The voice was suddenly cut

off by a thump and a crash and the sound of something heavy—like a body—hitting the floor.

"Ahhh!" someone cried out.

Tesla bolted down the stairs. "Come on! Uncle Newt's in trouble!"

"Are you sure that was Uncle Newt?"

It was hard to tell men's voices apart when they were just screaming, in Nick's opinion.

Still, he followed his sister as she whipped around the bottom of the banister and charged up the hall. He did take one precaution, though.

"Operator? I'd like to report an emergency," he said loudly, speaking into the nonexistent phone in his hand. "Someone's broken into our house, and all we have to protect ourselves is our uncle's shotgun and a flamethrower. Could you send backup?"

Nick hoped to hear something like "Let's get outta here!" from up ahead, but no such luck. He burst into the kitchen behind Tesla, expecting to find the nefarious Mr. Snugg waiting for them with half a dozen knuckle-cracking thugs.

Instead, when Tesla flipped on the light they found their uncle on the floor, half buried under cans of Beefaroni.

"I have a shotgun?" he said.

When he saw that Nick's hands were empty, he grinned and shook a finger at him.

"Nice bluff!"

"Where are they? Where are they?" said Tesla. She hurried to the back door—which was firmly closed—and peered out through the glass. "Did you fight them off? How many of them were there?"

"There were about three hundred of them," Uncle Newt said. He started sweeping Beefaroni cans off his chest and legs. "And I didn't fight them off. They just fell on me."

Nick bent down next to his uncle and helped him dig himself out.

"You mean . . . you haven't seen anyone?" Tesla said.

"Our alarm light came on," Nick explained. "We got an intruder alert."

"'An intruder alert'? I love it! It's like we're in an episode of *Star Trek*." Uncle Newt pushed himself to his feet and then squinted down at Nick. "Do you guys know what *Star Trek* is?"

"We know," Nick said.

"But we heard voices," Tesla protested. "Right before the big crash."

"Oh, that was just me talking to myself," Uncle Newt said. "I got steamed because I'm hung up on this bioluminescent Christmas tree I've been tinkering with. The needles keep wanting to glow brown. I mean, come on! Is there a less Christmas-y color? I was so cheesed I forgot I had all this stuff piled up in here. When I came up to go to bed, I walked smack into a stack of Beefaroni."

"Did you open the back door before you fell?" Tesla asked. "To let the cat out or something?"

"Oh, no. Eureka's been strictly an indoor cat ever since his fur fell out. Don't get me started on *that* debacle. Sandy Paws, the Christmas kitty litter that glows red and green . . . and makes your cat go bald by Christmas Eve. Oops. Bioluminescents are really *not* my strong suit."

"But, Uncle Newt—the alarm light was on," Tesla said. "Someone opened this door."

Uncle Newt looked around the kitchen, his eyes wide. "Who, Tesla? I don't see anybody. It must have been a nightmare."

"We both saw the light," Nick pointed out.

Uncle Newt shrugged. "A short circuit, then."

Tesla's expression darkened. It was one thing to tell her she was imagining things. But tell her she'd screwed up her circuitry? Watch out.

Uncle Newt didn't seem to notice. He just spread his arms wide and started shooing Nick and Tesla toward the hall.

"Come on. Back to bed. It's the middle of the night, and don't kids need, like, twenty hours of sleep a day?"

"I think that's dogs," said Nick.

Tesla just crossed her arms over her chest, stuck out her chin, and allowed herself to be herded up the stairs.

"I know you guys are a little on edge after what happened with that SUV," Uncle Newt said as Nick and Tesla got back in bed. "But really, you have nothing to worry about. You're safe as can be here. Truly. Now good night."

"Good night," said Nick.

Tesla simply grunted.

Uncle Newt turned out the light and left.

"You've got to admit," Nick said. "It *could* have been a short circuit."

"It wasn't."

"Well, there's not much we can do about it now, unless you want to go back downstairs and check . . . the . . . oh, man."

"What?"

Nick made himself get out of bed.

"Would you come with me, please?" he said to his sister. "And not let me turn around and run back and hide under the covers?"

"Do you have to go to the bathroom?"

"No! Geez, Tez! I have to go back to the kitchen."

"Why?"

Nick swallowed. Hard.

"I know how we can prove it wasn't a short circuit."

Tesla was instantly on her feet.

"Let's go," she said.

Nick wanted to be wrong. He wanted Tesla to be wrong. He wanted the alarm to have short-circuited. Better to have made a mistake, in this case, than to be right.

He crossed the kitchen with slow, hesitant steps

that would have been even more slow and hesitant—or fast and certain, but in the opposite direction—if Tesla hadn't been behind him.

When he reached the back door, he looked down at the coins and wires taped to the floor. The little piece of paper that had separated the coins wasn't between them anymore. Instead, it was about four inches away.

Maybe Uncle Newt had pulled it out accidentally, his foot scuffing over the coins as he walked through the kitchen in the dark. There was one way to find out.

Nick wrapped a sweaty hand around the door-knob, turned, and pushed.

The door opened.

It was unlocked.

Nick quickly pulled the door shut again. Then he locked it . . . for all the good that would do.

He'd locked it—and double-checked and triple-checked that he'd locked it—before he and Tesla had first gone upstairs to bed.

"That means someone picked the lock and got inside, but got scared off when Uncle Newt came up from the lab," Tesla said. "And because they were in a hurry to get away—"

"They didn't have time to *re*lock the door," Nick said.

His voice was trembling, and it bothered him. Tesla always sounded so confident when she finished his sentences for him.

He cleared his throat and took a big step away from the door.

"So," he said, his voice strong and steady. Or a little stronger and steadier, anyway. He hoped. "What do we do now?"

"Step one," Tesla said.

She walked off to the living room, then returned with one of the dusty chairs their uncle had retrieved from his garage earlier that evening. (Tesla had announced that eating "astronaut style" wasn't going to work for her. Ever.) She took the chair to the door and wedged it up under the knob, turning it into a crude but effective brace.

"Sometimes the old-fashioned ways are best," she said, looking extremely pleased with herself.

"What's step two?" Nick asked.

"That should be obvious," Tesla told him. "We end this."

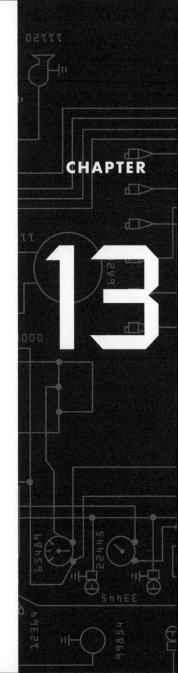

The next morning, Tesla and Nick outlined their plan to Silas and De-Marco. They were all hiding out in Uncle Newt's backyard at the time, partially to avoid the black SUV and/or Mr. Snugg, partially to avoid DeMarco's little sister Elesha. (The girl had vowed to make Nick pay for crashing her bicycle, and it wasn't clear whether she meant "pay" with money or pain. DeMarco was of the opinion that it would probably be both.)

"So, after getting threatened and chased and almost torn apart by dogs the size of dinosaurs," Silas

NICK AND TESLA'S HIGH-VOLTAGE DANGER LAB

said, "you not only want go back to the old Landrigan place, you want to go inside?"

Nick just nodded. When Silas put it like that, it was hard to work up much enthusiasm.

Tesla managed it, though.

"Yes," she said firmly. "Did you tell your parents about the weirdness going on there? About the girl and her message?"

Silas and DeMarco nodded.

"And did they do anything?" Tesla asked.

"They just said she was probably Vince's or Frank's daughter," said Silas.

"Or some rich, snooty Landrigan kid," said DeMarco.

"See?" Tesla said to Nick. "Occam's razor again."

"Whoa!" Silas blurted out. "Who's got a razor?"

"It's just an expression," Nick said. "It describes a way of thinking. Avoiding overly complicated explanations. Usually it's helpful, but—"

"What if the truth *is* complicated?" Tesla cut in. "And what if that girl really is in trouble? Someone's got to find out."

"And that someone is you?" DeMarco asked.

"Who else?" Tesla said.

There was a loud thump and the ground shook

and the kids could hear the muffled sound of coughing and cursing.

Uncle Newt was still having trouble with his kiln. It was all he'd been able to talk about that morning.

Silas and DeMarco turned to look at each other as little wisps of smoke curled out around Uncle Newt's back door.

"Going back to the Landrigan place? With those dogs there and that SUV prowling around?" Silas said. "Sounds like suicide."

"Totally," said DeMarco. "But then again . . . what else were we gonna do today?"

Silas shrugged. "Just ride around."

They faced Nick and Tesla again.

"We're in," they said.

Silas's job would be distracting the dogs.

"We can build you something that'll help," Tesla said. "We'll only need an hour or so."

"And a trip to a store," Nick said. "We're out of Mentos."

"*Mentos?*" DeMarco said.

"Sure. Let me show you."

Tesla picked up the notebook they'd been writing their plan in and began drawing a diagram of the mint-and-cola-powered RoboSquirrel. Silas stopped her after she'd reached step five of the construction process.

"Here," he said, taking the pen and paper from her, "let me sketch out *my* idea."

Nick nodded, impressed. "It'll take a lot less time and effort to build, and I bet it works just as well as RoboSquirrel." He turned to his sister. "Do you ever get the feeling we overthink things?"

Tesla didn't answer him.

"What's up with the eagle?" she asked instead.

"He just likes drawing eagles," DeMarco explained.

"So? Should I get the bologna?" Silas asked Tesla.

"Sure. And the string," she said. "But don't let anyone see you bringing them back here."

"Don't worry! I'm like a ninja!" Silas called out as he dashed away. "Too fast for the human eye to . . . oh. Hi, Mrs. Casserly."

Uncle Newt's neighbor Julie was standing in her yard, arms folded across her chest, glaring at them.

"Don't worry, ma'am!" Nick said to her. "We're not doing anything explosive today! Promise!"

Julie just kept glaring.

DeMarco turned his back to her.

"What about me?" he said. "What's my job?"

"You're going to be more bologna," Nick told him.

"What?"

"Another distraction—and one that's just as important," Tesla said. "Those attack dogs aren't the only thing between us and the girl that's vicious and nasty."

The kids didn't have watches to synchronize when they split up, so they decided to just start counting and hope that they all got to one hundred at more or less the same time.

Silas went to the north side of the fence around the Landrigan place. Nick and Tesla went to the south side of the fence. DeMarco went to the gate.

"Seventy-seven," said Nick as he and Tesla crept closer to the fence. "Seventy-eight. Seventy-nine."

Far away, they could hear dogs barking and snarling as only Rottweilers fighting over old lunch meat can.

"Silas must be a fast counter," Nick said.

"Well, we may as well go then," said Tesla. "That bologna won't last forever."

She moved to the fence and started climbing. Nick was right behind her.

Once they were on the ground on the other

side, they darted toward the Landrigans' mansion. A bark stopped Nick cold as they crossed the driveway. It wasn't coming from the far side of the yard, on the other side of the house, where Silas was supposed to be.

"Listen," Nick hissed at his sister.

Tesla stopped and cocked an ear.

The dog barked again. The sound was muted, yet close.

Nick and Tesla turned toward the garage behind the house. More muffled barks rang out from inside it.

"I heard that dog back there last time I was here," Nick said. "I guess Jaws and Claws have backup."

"Yeah, but he's locked up for some reason, so we don't have to worry about him," said Tesla.

She started toward the house again.

"Well, maybe we don't *have* to worry about him," Nick muttered as he followed her. "But I think I will anyway, thank you."

Tesla shushed him.

Up ahead, someone else was talking.

Nick and Tesla reached the side of the old house and peeked cautiously around the corner.

No one was there. A window was half open—it was a warm day—and voices were coming from inside.

"—practically flattened me when that van of yours came zooming out into the street," DeMarco was saying, his voice loud and squawky and staticky. "My mom says we might sue."

He was talking over the intercom from the gate, just as they'd planned.

Tesla sneaked under the window and started to stand to peek through it. Nick waved his hands and shook his head and mouthed "NO . . . NO . . . NO," but his sister ignored him.

She ducked down again after looking inside for all of a second.

"Vince and Frank," she whispered. "They're both just standing there."

"Well, they've gotta move or we can't go in," Nick whispered back.

Tesla rolled her eyes. "Yeah. I know."

The whole time, DeMarco kept jabbering away over the intercom.

"I mean, my knee got scraped up real bad, and the paint chipped on my bike. But you know what? We might be willing to forgive your recklessness if you were to buy me a new bike and throw in . . . oh, let's say five hundred dollars for pain and suffering. Did I mention my back's been hurting ever since it happened? And my neck? Ohhhhh, it's starting to act up right now. The pain!"

"I'll give that brat a pain in the neck," Vince snarled.

"I swear, he looked fine when I left," Frank said. "He just fell is all. The van didn't touch him."

"You should've told me about it."

"I didn't think it was a big deal."

"*You should have told me.*"

"We haven't filed a police report yet," DeMarco went on. "Maybe we won't have to . . . if you do the right thing. Come on. How much does a bike cost, anyway?"

"He's bluffing," Frank said.

"It doesn't matter," Vince snapped back. "We can't have him out there yakking at us all day. Not when we're so close to finally finishing this thing."

"Well, what do we do? Run him off or play nice?"

"Nice would be better. We don't want any fuss. Not now. Not today."

"But, Vince . . . do you even *do* nice?"

"Not really. But I'm willing to try. Come on."

There were loud, clomping, echoing footsteps. As they faded away, Tesla stood for another look in the window. This time, Nick peeped in, too.

Just beyond the window was what must have been the kitchen, once upon a time. There was a rusty sink and an ancient stove and a cobweb-covered space between the faded cabinets and stained, chipped countertop where a refrigerator had probably stood.

More important, though, was what *wasn't* there: Vince and Frank.

Somewhere else in the house, a door creaked open and then slammed shut.

Vince and Frank were on their way to the front gate.

"Well, one thing's for sure," Nick said. "If those guys are fixing up the house, they did *not* start in the kitchen."

Tesla grunted, then turned and started toward the back door nearby.

"We've gotta move fast," she said. "We've probably only got a couple minutes before . . . oh, great."

She had her hand on the doorknob, which wasn't turning. The back door was locked.

"Through the window," Tesla said, whipping around and rushing back the way she'd just come. "Hurry."

"Hurry?" said Nick.

He'd never climbed through a kitchen window slowly. How was he supposed to hurry?

He got his head and arms through the window, then tried a jump that landed him on his chest on the sill. He started wiggling and kicking his legs, but he could feel himself sliding out again.

"Oh, come *on*," he heard Tesla groan, and there was a sudden pressure on his butt that lifted him up and forward.

"Hey!" Nick said as he slid over the sill and the sink and went plummeting to the floor. He just barely managed to hit the grungy old linoleum hands-first, not head-first.

"Thanks a lot," he grumbled as he stood up and dusted himself off.

Tesla was already slithering in after him.

"You're welcome," she said. "Little help?"

Nick grabbed his sister's hands and helped her

land more gracefully than he had.

"Stairs?" he said once she was firmly on her feet.

"Stairs."

They set off in search of a staircase.

The girl—assuming she was in the same room as before—would be exactly one floor above the kitchen.

Nick and Tesla passed through what was probably a dining room, to judge by its proximity to the kitchen and the grimy low-hanging chandelier. Someone had even been dining in it lately. The floor was littered with crumpled beer cans, empty potato chip bags, and plastic wrappers for beef jerky and cheap convenience store sandwiches.

"Classy," Nick said.

The dark hallway beyond was in even worse shape. Loose floorboards squeaked under their feet, chunks of fallen plaster from the ceiling were heaped here and there like snow, and the washed-out wallpaper was peeling away in big curling strips. The foyer and spiral staircase they found at the other end of the hall were every bit as ramshackle.

There were no tools in sight. Nothing seemed to have been repaired or restored or even so much as dusted.

Nick and Tesla passed a little portable TV as they headed for the stairs. Near it was a deck of cards spread out on the floor for a game of solitaire.

"Hey," Nick said. "You can't play the five of spades on the six of clubs."

"Someone who'd cheat at solitaire is capable of anything," Tesla said ominously.

Nick couldn't tell if she was joking or not.

"This way," Tesla said when they got to the top of the stairs.

"I know, I know."

They started down another dark plaster-pocked hall. At the end of it, at last, was some sign of renovations. Weird ones.

There was a shiny new latch on the hallway's last door. And a small hole, about the size of a silver dollar, had been drilled through the wall nearby. Sunshine streamed through it from the room beyond, creating a thin shaft of radiance that cut through the gloom like a little spotlight.

When Nick and Tesla reached the end of the hall, they both moved to look through the hole.

Before they could start arguing about who got to

go first, an eye appeared, squinting out at *them*.

"Yah!" Nick yelped.

"Eeahh!" someone else shrieked.

"Shhhhhhh!" said Tesla.

The eye disappeared. A moment later, though, it was back.

"You shouldn't have come in here. You're going to ruin everything."

It was a girl's voice, quiet and quavering.

Tesla reached out toward the latch. As she unhooked it, she and Nick looked at each other.

The girl had been locked in. There could be no doubt now: Frank and Vince were indeed bad, *bad* guys.

"Don't worry," Tesla said. "We're here to help you."

She opened the door.

The room beyond was almost empty. All that was in it was a ratty blanket, a pillow, a radio, a notepad, and a pen.

And the girl, of course. She was still in the nightgown she'd been wearing the first time Nick had seen her. She looked even skinnier and more pale up close.

"But what about Mr. Snugg?" she said.

"Don't worry," Tesla told her. "He went down to the

front gate. If we hurry, we'll be out of here before he gets back."

"Which one is he, anyway?" Nick asked. "Frank or Vince?"

The girl looked mystified.

"What are you talking about?" she said. "Mr. Snugg's locked up somewhere, like me. We have to find him."

"Wait," Nick said. "*What?*"

"Nick! Tesla! Run!" someone shouted behind them.

Nick and Tesla spun around.

Vince and Frank stood at the top of the stairs.

DeMarco was between them, one of the big men's meaty hands on each of his slight shoulders.

"Shut up, kid," Vince sneered. He shoved DeMarco toward his friends. "There's nowhere to run to anyway."

14

Vince was right. They were trapped. All Nick and Tesla could do was watch as Vince and Frank herded DeMarco down the hallway.

"I tried being nice," Vince said, giving DeMarco another push. "But this kid just wouldn't shut up. Wouldn't go away. And now I see why."

Vince shook his bald head. Nick could tell what he was thinking.

He was through being nice. It wasn't his strong suit, anyway.

A final shove sent DeMarco into the room with Nick and Tesla and the girl. He looked scared but unhurt.

"There any more little snoopers out there?" Frank asked.

"No!" Nick and Tesla blurted out at the same time.

Vince scoffed and jerked his head at DeMarco. "Yeah. That's what *he* said. Frank, get Jaws and Claws and take a look. If you see anyone else sneaking around, we should probably go ahead and wrap things up here. You follow?"

Frank nodded. To judge by the grim expression on his face, he followed all right—all the way to something extremely unpleasant.

He turned and stomped away.

Vince stayed behind, blocking the doorway to the girl's room. He blocked it well. He wasn't as muscle-bound as Frank, but he wasn't small either, and there was an intensity about him that seemed to buzz and crackle like an electric current. To Nick, he seemed like the sort of person you could hang signs on.

HIGH VOLTAGE

DANGER

BEWARE OF PSYCHO

"Why'd you have to stick your noses in now?" Vince said. "Just a couple more hours, and it'd all be over. Oh, well. It'll still be over in a couple hours. It's just a little more complicated now. But we'll smooth all that out . . . one way or another."

Vince tried a smile, but it came out crooked. It didn't look like he'd had much practice with them.

"Just sit tight and keep quiet, and everything'll work out fine," he said.

He closed the door, and Nick could hear him drop the latch back into place and stalk off down the hall.

"Work out fine for him and Frank, he means," Tesla said.

"What do you mean?" said DeMarco.

Nick knew better than to ask. He could *feel* what the answer was, and it made him shiver.

Tesla turned to the girl. "Okay. Who are you, and why is Vince keeping you and Mr. Snugg prisoner here?"

The girl slumped to the floor and sat, legs crossed, back hunched, head hung low. Maybe for a second or two she'd allowed herself to hope, but obviously that was over now.

"My name's Lily Lawrence. Vince and Frank kidnapped me five days ago. They're holding me for ransom. They want a million dollars."

"Whoa," said DeMarco. "You must be rich."

Lily Lawrence shrugged listlessly. "Yeah, I guess."

"Is Mr. Snugg from a rich family, too?" Nick asked.

"In a way. His full name is Mr. Alonzo Morningstar Snugglesgood. He's my Chihuahua."

Tesla slapped a hand to her forehead. "'The mastermind,'" she groaned. "A dog."

"They took him when they took me," Lily said. "Told me if I tried to escape or didn't cooperate, they'd feed him to their Rottweilers."

"Hey!" Nick said. "He must be the dog in the garage!"

Lily nodded sadly. "That's him. Vince and Frank say all they have to do is open the garage door and whistle for Jaws and Claws and . . . no more Mr. Snugg."

"What I don't get," DeMarco said, "is why your family hasn't just paid the ransom. Don't they want you back?"

Before he knew what he was doing, Nick was punching DeMarco on the shoulder.

"Nice one, Mr. Sensitive," he said.

"Hey!" DeMarco started rubbing his shoulder. "It's a fair question."

"For your information, my parents have been *trying* to pay the ransom," Lily told DeMarco. "A million dollars is a lot of money, though. You can't just go to the ATM for it. There's all kind of things you have to do to get that much cash, even when you're rich. That's why Vince and Frank have had to keep me here so long."

Tesla nodded along as Lily spoke, as if she knew everything the girl was going to say before she said it.

"Frank's trips out every night—that was to talk to your parents," Tesla said. "He had to go someplace new every time and use a disposable cell phone so no one could trace the call."

"Yes, exactly," Lily said, looking impressed. "He's been taking me with him, locked up in the back of the van. That way I could talk to Mom and Dad and let them know I'm not . . . you know."

Tesla was nodding again.

"And while Vince and Frank waited for the money, they kept you in the perfect hideout," she said. "A nice, big, abandoned house all to themselves, with no one around who might accidentally see you."

"Except she *was* seen," Nick said.

"And Vince and Frank have been seen, too," said Tesla. "By all of us. Which means we can describe them to the police."

"But they promised to let me go once they get the money," said Lily.

Tesla gave the girl a dubious look.

DeMarco finally caught on.

"Oh, man," he groaned, voice trembling. "What are we gonna do?"

Nick put a hand on DeMarco's shoulder, the same one he'd punched a minute before.

"Maybe Silas will bring help," he said.

"Yeah, maybe . . . if Vince and Frank don't catch him first," said DeMarco.

Tesla walked to the room's one window.

Nick shook his head. "We're up too high to jump. And the roof slants too much to crawl out onto."

Tesla turned and stared at the tattered old blanket on the floor.

Again, Nick read her mind. She was thinking of pulling the old Rapunzel routine.

"That blanket's not big enough or long enough to get us to the ground," Nick said. "And there's nothing in here to tie it to, anyway."

"Little Mr. Sunshine," Tesla muttered. But apparently she agreed with him.

She walked to the door and looked out through the hole drilled into the wall beside it.

"They use that to watch me," Lily explained. "Like, every time they bring me food, they make sure I'm standing on the far side of the room before they open the door. As if I'd try to jump out and karate chop them or something."

Tesla began poking and probing the plaster around the hole.

"This house may be falling apart, but that wall's solid as a rock," Lily said. "You won't be able to make that hole any bigger. And you can't get your hand through it, either. Believe me, I've tried. We're stuck in here."

"Little *Miss* Sunshine," Tesla said. She peered out through the hole again. "That latch. It's so close. If only we had a coat hanger or . . ."

Tesla spun around, suddenly beaming. There wasn't a shining light bulb over her head, but there might as well have been.

She pointed at the stuff on the floor beside the

blanket: the notepad, the pen, and the radio.

"Where'd that come from?"

"Vince and Frank gave it to me so I'd have something to do," Lily said. "I was so bored up here all day I started singing to myself, and I think it got on their nerves."

Tesla rushed over and practically pounced on the radio. She snatched it up, flipped it over, and popped off the plastic lid on the back.

"Yes! Batteries! And I bet there's some wire in here we could pull out, too."

"Good one, Tez!" Nick said. "But we'll need some metal."

He started pacing around the room, stopping every so often to bounce up and down when he found a particularly loose floorboard.

"A nail," he said. "A nail. A nail. A . . . a-ha!"

One of the floorboards bowed so much in the middle it practically made a U. Rusty, blackened nails protruded from each end.

"What the heck could batteries, wire, and old nails be good for?" DeMarco asked.

Nick and Tesla just looked at each other, smiling grimly. Then they showed him.

TESLA AND NICK'S
DO-IT-YOURSELF
ELECTROMAGNET AND
PICKER-UPPER

THE STUFF:

- 1 D-size battery

- 1 strand of 24-gauge plastic-coated wire

- 1 3- to 4-inch (7.5 to 10-cm) iron or steel nail

- Tape

- Wire strippers or scissors

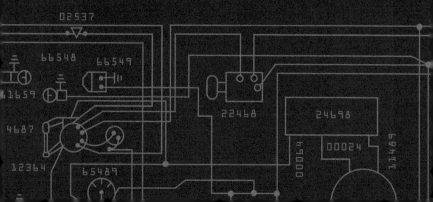

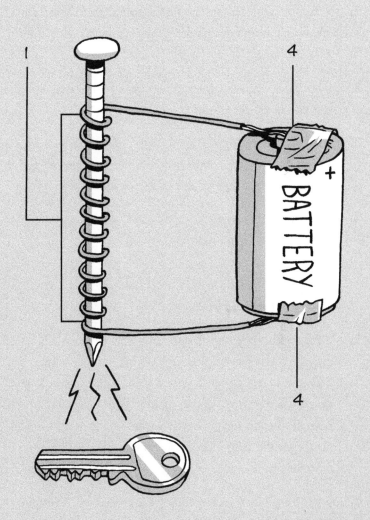

THE SETUP

1. Wrap the wire around the nail, leaving about 8 inches (20.5 cm) loose at one end. Try not to let the ends of the wire overlap.

2. If necessary, cut the wire so that about 8 inches (20.5 cm) is loose at the other end, too.

3. Using the wire strippers or scissors, remove ½ inch (1.25 cm) of the plastic coating from both ends of the wire. Ask an adult if you have trouble with this step.

4. Tape one exposed end of the wire to the top of the battery and the other to the bottom.

THE FINAL STEPS

1. Once the battery's connected, the flow of electricity through the wires creates an invisible magnetic field. The nail is now a magnet, and you should be able to pick up small metal objects with it, such as paper clips or nuts and bolts. The more times you wrap the wire around the nail, the larger the magnetic field and thus the stronger the magnetic force.

2. Don't forget to disconnect the wires when you're done. The wires and nail will get very hot over extended use, so *never* leave the electromagnet assembled!

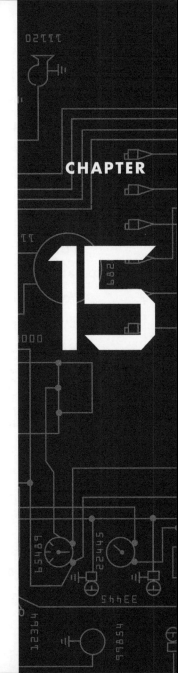

15

Getting the nail and wires through the peephole in the wall was the easy part. The hard part was getting them to snake around to the left and unhook the latch locking the door.

The kids knew that the electro-magnet worked. They'd tested it on the other nail they'd managed to pry from the loose floorboard. But after fiddling with the wires for five minutes, the side of her face smooshed against the wall and her tongue sticking out, Tesla gave up.

"I don't think I'm getting the right angle," she said. "You give it a try, Nick. But watch out. The wire's getting—"

Nick took the battery from his sister and immediately said, "Yipe!"

"—hot," Tesla finished.

Nick tried for five minutes, but he couldn't get the nail attached to the latch.

DeMarco tried for five minutes, but he couldn't get the nail attached to the latch, either.

"I think I can do it," said Lily. "I'm really good at Operation."

"You mean . . . the game?" DeMarco said.

Lily nodded.

DeMarco looked back at Nick and Tesla.

They each gave him a "Why not?" shrug.

"All right," said DeMarco, letting Lily take the battery from his hand. "But this is a lot harder than taking out the funny bone without lighting up the guy's—"

"Got it," Lily said.

"Got it?" said Nick.

"Yeah. Got it. At least I think I got it. I felt a tug, as if the nail had suddenly moved itself. Then I gave a little pull, and something seemed to shift."

"That sure was fast," DeMarco said, looking unconvinced.

"That's how I work," Lily said.

Nick stepped to the door and reached for the knob.

"Well, there's an easy way to find out if the latch is still in the hook or not," he said.

He turned the knob and pushed.

The door swung open.

"Oh," said DeMarco. "Good one."

He held up his hand toward Lily, and they high-fived.

"So what do we do now?" Lily said.

Tesla stretched out an arm toward the dark hallway. "We leave."

"You make it sound so easy," Nick said.

"Maybe it will be."

Nick gave his sister a glum deadpan glare.

"Come on," she said.

She started down the hall with slow, soft steps.

They reached the top of the staircase without hearing anyone or (so far as they could tell) being heard themselves.

"They're probably still out searching the grounds for other kids," Lily whispered.

"Let's hope they don't find any," said Nick.

They'd need a lot of luck just to escape. But to escape *and* rescue Silas? That would require more luck than you need to win the lottery.

Tesla led the way down the stairs and then across the dusty, musty foyer to the front door. There were narrow floor-to-ceiling windows on either side of the door, and the kids wiped the grime off the glass just enough to peek outside.

The front gate to the Landrigan estate was about forty yards away, at the bottom of a gently sloping hill overgrown with weeds and waist-high grass.

Vince and Frank and Jaws and Claws were nowhere in sight.

"So, now we just run for it?" Nick said.

"Would you rather walk?" said Tesla.

Nick nodded. "Right. Run it is."

"On the count of three?" Tesla said.

DeMarco and Lily nodded, too.

"Okay," said Tesla. "One. Two. Three!"

Tesla threw open the door, and all four kids rocketed out of the house and onto the lawn.

They weren't a dozen strides onto the grass before they heard a gruff voice off to the far left call out "Hey!" Then, just a few strides later, there was more to hear—barking and growling and the sound of huge bodies moving fast through the grass. The kids looked toward the noise and saw what they expected. And dreaded.

Jaws and Claws were charging their way, covering the ground between them with terrifying speed.

The kids weren't fast enough. They wouldn't make it to the gate.

Lily screamed. Nick might have, too. He wasn't sure. He was too scared.

Instinctively, all four kids turned their backs to the big dogs, veering off to the right.

They were running for the fence now. Maybe—*maybe*—one or two of them could climb up and over and get away. But there was no way all of them would.

The Rottweilers were finally going to use the jaws and claws they'd been named for.

The fence was just twenty yards away. Then ten. Then five. Then Nick and Tesla and DeMarco and Lily were lined up against it, all of them looking back to

see why they were alive.

Jaws and Claws were still closing in on them. But slowly now, heads down, snarling, frothing. When they were a little less than a dozen feet from the kids, they stopped and just stood there.

"Why don't they finish us?" DeMarco said. "What are they waiting for?"

"The signal," Tesla said. "From them."

Vince and Frank came striding up behind the dogs.

"Un-be-lievable," Vince grated out through gritted teeth. "On the last day. *The last day.*" He jabbed a finger at Lily. "You. Move away from the others."

Lily just blinked at him, still panting from her dash across the yard.

"I said *move!*" Vince barked.

"Why?" Lily asked.

"Because he needs you on the phone one more time before he gets his money," Tesla said. "Right, Vince? Me and Nick and DeMarco you can get rid of now, but Lily you need . . . for another hour or so."

Vince looked like he wanted to chomp into Tesla and rip her to shreds without any help from his dogs.

"Shut up."

"We gotta hurry it up, Vince," Frank said nervously. "If we're gonna do something out in the open like this, we gotta get it over with, know what I mean?"

"Yeah. I sure do."

For the second time, Nick saw Vince smile. This one wasn't an I'm-trying-to-look-nice smile, though. It was an I'm-going-to-enjoy-this smile. And this time, he seemed to mean it.

Vince glanced to the right, obviously looking for potential witnesses in the field on the other side of the fence. When he didn't see any, he glanced to the left, toward the street.

His smile disappeared.

"What in the—"

There was a roar and a squeal and a crash, and something smashed through the Landrigans' front gate and zoomed up the drive.

It was a big black SUV.

As it swerved toward Nick, Tesla, DeMarco, and Lily, they could do nothing but press back against the fence behind them and stare in shock. Jaws and Claws went darting away whimpering, and Frank stumbled backward, tripped over his own feet, and ended up flat on his back. Only Vince stood his ground as the SUV bore down on them.

At the last second, it screeched to a halt.

The driver's side door flew open, and a red-haired woman in a dark pantsuit and sunglasses popped out. She had a gun in her hand.

She pointed it at Vince.

"Down on the ground!"

Vince stole a peek at his dogs. They were trotting back toward the SUV now, growling uncertainly.

"Keep those dogs back and get yourself flat on the ground *now!*" the woman snapped.

Vince stared down the barrel of the woman's gun for a moment, then heaved a heavy sigh.

"Jaws. Claws. Sit. Stay," he said.

The dogs obeyed.

Vince went down to his knees and then stretched out flat on the grass.

"The last day," he was muttering. "The last day."

The woman shifted her steely gaze to Frank. "You. Roll over on your face like your friend. Hands and feet apart."

Frank was as obedient as Jaws and Claws.

Lily ran toward the woman, tears in her eyes.

"Thank you, thank you, thank you!" she cried. "I knew the police would find me sooner or later!"

There was a whirring sound from the SUV. Someone was rolling down the window behind the driver's seat.

A grinning Silas poked out his head.

"Oh, she's not a cop," he said to Lily. "And she wasn't looking for you. She was looking for them."

He pointed at Nick and Tesla.

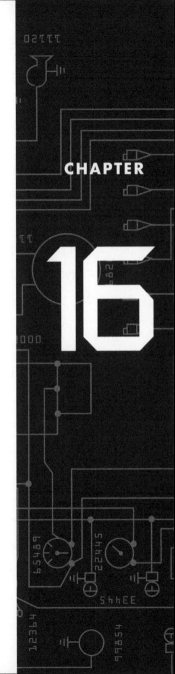

CHAPTER

16

"Wait," Nick said. "Looking for *us*? Why?"

The red-headed woman snaked her left hand into one of her pockets. Without taking her eyes (or gun) off Vince and Frank, she pulled out a necklace and tossed it to Tesla.

"My pendant!" Tesla said.

She immediately put the necklace back on.

"Don't lose it again," the woman said. Her short hair and clenched jaw and narrowed eyes made her look stern, but there might have been a hint of a smile twisting her thin lips.

"I've got your rocket, too. But you probably don't want it back. It's pretty much just chewed-up plastic and dog slobber."

Nick looked back and forth between the woman and his sister. "But how . . . ? When . . . ? Who . . . ?"

"Your mother and father are friends of mine," the woman said. "That's all I can tell you."

"But . . . but . . . but . . . ."

In the distance, sirens wailed. Lots of them.

Jaws—or maybe it was Claws—began howling along.

Vince and Frank popped their faces up out of the grass.

"The last day," Vince groaned as the sirens grew louder. "The last day."

"Oh, shut up," Frank snapped.

It was unclear whether he was talking to Vince or the dog.

"But . . . I don't understand," Nick said to the woman. He looked at her gun. "You're not a cop?"

"No, I'm not," the woman said. "But I am . . . associated with the police, in a way. I called them before I drove in here." She jerked her head sideways, at Silas. "You can thank your friend for filling me in on what you've been up to. Until I talked to him, I had no idea just how much trouble you were in. I think your mom and dad are going to be a little disappointed in all of us."

"But why would . . . ? How did you . . . ? Have you been . . . ?"

"*That's all I can tell you,*" the woman said again. Her voice was firm but not harsh, and she looked at Nick with a twinkle in her eyes that seemed to say, "Maybe next time, kid."

Three San Mateo County Sheriff's cruisers came whooshing through the Landrigans' busted gate. Not far behind were a pair of California Highway Patrol motorcycles, an Animal Control truck, an ambulance, and, bringing up the rear, a dinky three-wheeled meter reader's car.

"Whoa!" said Silas.

"It's everyone but the National Guard," said De-Marco.

The woman might have only been "associated" with the police "in a way," but obviously when she called, they listened.

A small swarm of police officers rushed past her SUV, and Vince and Frank were quickly surrounded and handcuffed.

The woman lowered her gun, and one of the cops—a balding, sixtyish man in a rumpled suit who'd climbed out of the meter reader three-wheeler—turned to her and said, "Thank you, Agent McIntyre. We'll take it from here."

The woman threw a sly look at Nick and Tesla.

"Pretend you didn't hear that," she said to them.

A moment later, all five kids—Nick, Tesla, De-Marco, Lily, and Silas—were being herded into squad cars for what the balding cop called "a little trip downtown."

"You're taking us to jail?" DeMarco wailed.

"What?" the cop said. "No! No, no, no!" He paused to think it over. "Well, technically, yes."

DeMarco moaned.

"Just so I can get your statements," the cop said. "Don't worry. I'll call your moms and dads and tell them where you are."

"Call . . . our . . . *moms?*" DeMarco croaked.

He and Silas turned to each other, their eyes wide.

"It's been nice knowin' ya, bro," Silas said.

"Right back at ya, dude," said DeMarco.

They hugged, looking like they were about to cry.

Nick and Tesla barely noticed. They were both watching the black SUV drive off up the street.

The balding cop was named Sergeant Feiffer, and he brought each of the kids watery hot chocolate as he interviewed them one by one in a meeting room at Half Moon Bay police headquarters. All the other cops had left after dropping off Vince and Frank in the little building's one holding cell.

It turned out that Sergeant Feiffer pretty much *was* the Half Moon Bay police force. The other cops had been on loan from the county sheriff and the Highway Patrol. The only other person in the office after they were gone was an ancient administrative assistant named Yvonne who pecked at her computer keyboard at a pace somewhere around a letter a minute and wore her hair in a big beehive that looked like a giant white swirl of vanilla ice cream on her head.

When Sergeant Feiffer seemed to be wrapping up his interview with her, Tesla asked if he was really the town's only cop.

"These days, yeah," he said ruefully. "We used to have a chief, two uniforms, and a meter reader, but then the economy went"—he turned a thumb downward and blew a raspberry. "Oh, well. It's not like we have much crime around here, anyway. Even Hutchings and Garratt were from out of town."

"Who?"

"That's the guys you caught. Vince Hutchings and Frank Garratt. Couple two-bit lowlifes out of Sacramento. I guess this was supposed to be their shot at the big time."

"Sacramento. Of course," Tesla said, speaking to herself as much as to Sergeant Feiffer. "Where Siringo Bros. Home Renovators are located."

Sergeant Feiffer nodded, looking impressed. "Exactly. And they'll be glad to get their van back. I hope you don't mind, but I'm stealing all the credit, by the way. If the town council thought they could let kids solve every crime for free, why would they need me, am I right?"

When Tesla didn't laugh at his joke, Sergeant Feiffer laughed for her.

"Anywho," he said, looking back down at the forms he'd been filling out, "it seems Mr. Hutchings and Mr.

Garratt aren't the only lawbreakers in town today. You do know that trespassing is illegal, don't you?"

"Oh. Yes. I'm sorry. We didn't really think about that."

The sergeant looked back up at Tesla and smiled. "Don't worry. I think it can be overlooked this once."

"Did Agent McIntyre put in a good word for us?"

"Who?"

"Agent McIntyre. The woman who saved our lives."

Sergeant Feiffer scratched his bald head.

"McIntyre, McIntyre, McIntyre," he said. "Nope. Don't know anyone named McIntyre. We did get a tip about a disturbance on the Landrigan estate, but it was phoned in anonymously."

"But I definitely heard you call that woman—"

"Well, I'd say we're done here," Sergeant Feiffer cut in. "Thank you for all your help."

He gave Tesla a McGruff the Crime Dog coloring book and held out a hand toward the door.

Tesla had been the last of the kids to be interviewed. By the time she stepped out of the meeting room,

Silas and DeMarco were already gone, and Lily was being led away by an attractive teary-eyed couple.

Lily turned back when she heard the door open, and Tesla saw that she was cradling a little yellow-brown bundle in her arms.

The little yellow-brown bundle growled at her.

"Hello, Mr. Snugg," Tesla said.

"You're done! Good! I was worried I wouldn't get to talk to you again!" Lily said. She took a step toward Tesla, but Mr. Snugg started barking, so she stopped. "I wanted to thank you for everything. You were amazing! So brave, so smart. You're, like, my hero!"

Tesla's face grew strangely warm and tingly.

She didn't blush much, so she didn't even know what it felt like.

"Oh, well . . . you're welcome," she said with an awkward shrug.

"I can't tell you how grateful we are," said the man standing behind Lily—her father, obviously. "If there's anything we can ever do for you, just let us know."

"All right. Sure."

Lily lifted one of Mr. Snugg's paws and made him wave, even though he was still growling and baring his little teeth at Tesla.

"Good-bye!" she said.

Nick stepped up beside Tesla.

"Bye," they said together.

Lily and her mom and dad left, leaving Nick and Tesla alone with Yvonne the administrative assistant.

Yvonne was hunched over her keyboard, either hunting for a letter she couldn't find or dozing.

"So," Nick said, "how'd it go?"

"Okay, but weird."

"That's how it was for me. There's a lot that people haven't been telling us."

"I know. And unfortunately the only person we can turn to for answers is—"

The door that Lily and her parents had just walked through burst open again, and a grinning Uncle Newt came striding in.

"Hey, kids!" he said. "Who wants to grab a nice plate of oysters?"

Nick and Tesla had to explain that, although going out for seafood wasn't necessarily something they hated, it wasn't the sort of treat most traumatized eleven-year-olds could get excited about.

"I see," said Uncle Newt. "How about sushi?"

They ended up getting ice cream.

"So," Uncle Newt said once they were all hunkered down around a little round table in the local ice cream shop, "Bill tells me you two foiled a kidnapping or some such."

"Bill?" said Nick.

"Sergeant Feiffer. He's out to the house pretty regularly—checking on explosions and 'strange glows' and 'threats to public safety,' whatever that means—so we've gotten kind of chummy."

"Well, he's right," Nick said. "Although technically I guess we didn't foil the *kidnapping*. That happened before we got here. But we did help save the kidnapped girl and catch the kidnappers."

"Hey, better late than never," said Uncle Newt. "Tell me about it."

Nick looked at his sister. She was working methodically on her scoop of mint chocolate chip with a distant, slightly sullen look on her face.

Obviously, it was up to Nick to tell the story.

Uncle Newt listened politely enough, though he

got excited and asked questions only when Nick was describing the gadgets and doohickeys he and Tesla had whipped up. It was as if he heard stories about kids facing down killer dogs and hardened criminals every day, but when they made their own squirrel out of diet cola and Mentos . . . now *that* was something!

"Well done, you two! I'm proud of you!" Uncle Newt said when the story was over. "An electromagnet built from a radio and rusty nails? I love it!"

"Thanks," said Nick. "Still . . . there are some unanswered questions."

"Oh?"

Nick gave Uncle Newt a significant look.

Uncle Newt stared back blankly. If there'd been a word balloon over his head, it would have looked like this:

Tesla finally broke her silence.

"Why are we really here?" she said.

Uncle Newt looked at her in surprise. "I thought we'd settled that. We're here to get ice cream."

"No," Tesla said. "Why are Nick and I in Half Moon Bay?"

"Well, you know that as well as I do, Tesla. Your mother and father are in Uzbekistan studying . . . studying . . . Brussels sprouts?"

"Soybeans," Nick said.

"And we don't believe that anymore," said Tesla.

Uncle Newt had his tongue out for a big lick of double fudge praline swirl.

He sucked his tongue back in.

"Don't believe it?" he said.

Tesla shook her head. "We've always been told that Mom and Dad were government scientists who specialize in agriculture. But the way they suddenly had to go running off to another country halfway around the world? It doesn't make sense."

"Oh, you might be surprised," Uncle Newt said. "The world of high-yield farming can be a roller-coaster ride of thrills and chills."

Tesla gave him an "Oh, puh-leeeeze" roll of the eyes.

He didn't seem to notice.

"A woman helped us today," said Nick. "Some kind of government agent. And she said she was a friend of Mom and Dad's."

"A friend they'd asked to check on us," Tesla added.

"Really?" Uncle Newt went ahead and took his bite of ice cream, then kept speaking as he moved it around in his mouth. "I wonder if I should be insulted. As if I'm not responsible enough to look after a couple kids!"

A little dab of double fudge praline swirl was stuck to his nose.

Tesla pulled out her pendant and showed it to her uncle. "Somehow, she found this even though we couldn't."

"That's the locket your Mom and Dad gave you?"

"We think it might be a tracking device," Nick said. "The woman—Agent McIntyre—she was the person following us around in the black SUV. She probably wanted to keep an eye on us because Tesla had lost her pendant."

"And last night, someone *did* try to get into the house," Tesla said. "I think it might have been Agent McIntyre again. We'd sneaked inside after the chase on the road, so she had no way of knowing I'd made it home safely. I think she wanted to check."

Uncle Newt put down what was left of his ice cream cone—laying it on its side on the table—and folded his arms across his chest.

"Let me see if I understand your hypothesis here," he said. "Your mother and father aren't in Uzbekistan studying lima beans—"

"Soybeans," said Nick.

"—but are really mixed up with some kind of secret agents? And they sent you here and had you put under surveillance because . . . ?"

"There's some kind of danger," Tesla said. "To them or Nick and me or all of us . . . we don't know."

"Which is why we're asking you," said Nick.

Uncle Newt shook his head, looking disappointed. "Kids, kids, kids. Don't you remember Occam's—"

Tesla cut him off.

"Occam's razor assumes that life tends to be simple," she said. "And sometimes it's not."

Uncle Newt stopped shaking his head and seemed to mull over her statement.

"You're right," he said eventually. "About Occam's razor, anyway. The rest of it . . . ?" He shrugged his bony shoulders. "It's hard to picture my brother hanging out with spies. And I've never been big on conspiracy theories. Well, except for the one about Elvis faking his death and living out the rest of his life in a trailer park. The *National Enquirer* ran some pretty convincing stuff on that, back in the day."

Uncle Newt picked up his cone again. About half the remaining double fudge praline swirl stayed behind, puddled on top of the table.

"Of course, that was ages ago," Uncle Newt said. He took a lick of ice cream and got another, even bigger splotch on his nose. "You kids have probably never heard of Elvis. He was a singer . . . and a great mind. Invented the fried peanut butter and banana sandwich, which is nothing to sneeze at. That's the only way I can eat bananas, in fact. If it weren't for Elvis sandwiches and candy apples, I'd probably never eat fruit at all."

Nick and Tesla looked at each other as Uncle Newt went on about his dislike of fresh fruit and the debt he owed Elvis.

On their first day in Half Moon Bay, Nick had joked that they'd been sent to stay with Uncle Newt because he was so clueless that he wouldn't ask awkward questions about where their parents were going or why.

It didn't seem like a joke anymore.

Uncle Newt did eventually remember Nick and Tesla's questions—and the fact that he hadn't provided any answers.

"Look," he said as they walked out of the ice cream shop, "I meant what I said about being proud of you. And it's not just because you know how to wire up your own intruder alert or use markers to follow cars. You're a couple of amazing kids who can handle more than most adults. Including me. So I wouldn't keep secrets from you. I mean . . . do I seem like the overprotective type?"

"No," said Nick.

"Quite the opposite," said Tesla.

Uncle Newt beamed at them. "See? So you can believe me when I say that your parents are not spies and that this kidnapping business and the agent lady and the other excitement you've had is just one big fluke. Really, guys—it's going to be a nice, quiet, *boring* summer from here on out. Okay?"

"Okay," said Nick.

"Okay," said Tesla.

"Good," said Uncle Newt. "Now, let's hurry up and get home. I've got a batch of barium nitrate cooking that'll go up like dynamite if I'm not back in my lab by . . ." He checked his watch. "Uh-oh."

Uncle Newt started walking a lot faster.

"Don't you mean *our* lab?" Tesla said as she and Nick scurried along beside him.

"Yes, yes! Of course! *Our* lab!" Uncle Newt said. He sped up into a sprint. "And we wouldn't want it to blow up, now would we?"

"No, Uncle Newt!" Nick and Tesla said together. Before they broke into a run, they looked at each other, obviously thinking the same thing.

A nice, quiet, boring summer? Yeah, right.

Tesla was smiling. Nick wasn't.

After that, they were so intent on catching up with their uncle that they didn't even notice the black sedan following them down the street or the drone airplane circling around and around and around high overhead. . . .

About the Authors

"SCIENCE BOB" PFLUGFELDER is an award-winning elementary school science teacher. His fun and informative approach to science has led to television appearances on the History Channel and *Access Hollywood*. He is also a regular guest on *Jimmy Kimmel Live*, *The Dr. Oz Show*, and *Live with Kelly & Michael*. Articles on Bob's experiments have appeared in *People*, *Nickelodeon* magazine, *Popular Science*, *Disney's Family Fun*, and *Wired*. He lives in Watertown, Massachusetts.

STEVE HOCKENSMITH is the author of the Edgar-nominated Holmes on the Range mystery series. His other books include the *New York Times* best seller *Pride and Prejudice and Zombies: Dawn of the Dreadfuls* and the short-story collection *Naughty: Nine Tales of Christmas Crime*. He lives with his wife and two children about forty minutes from Half Moon Bay, California.